SUPERNATURAL

THE OFFICIAL COOKBOOK

SUPERNATURAL

THE OFFICIAL COOKBOOK

BURGERS, PIES, AND OTHER
BITES FROM THE ROAD

Dean says, EAT MORE Pie! JOIN THE HUNT.

BY JULIE TREMAINE
PHOTOGRAPHY BY JESSICA TORRES

INSIGHT
EDITIONS

San Rafael · Los Angeles · London

CONTENTS

INTRODUCTION

The Winchesters have always been men of undeniably simple tastes. As the sons of hunters, Sam and Dean have grown up on the road, traveling from motel to motel in pursuit of the next case and the next person to save. It isn't a way of life that allows for much relaxation or for much cooking. From diners to bars to, well, more diners, the brothers have eaten their way across the country, tasting everything from barbecue to bacon dogs to what Dean calls "the best burger in the world."

Within these pages, you'll find food from *Supernatural*, both what the characters eat on the show and dishes inspired by those characters. There are plenty of ways to eat like the Winchesters—both Dean's indulgences and Sam's healthy choices—plus foods that take a page from Bobby, John and Mary, Castiel, Jack, Charlie, and Crowley. There's even a whole section devoted to the pies Dean desperately craves and hardly ever manages to eat. And in true *Supernatural* form, there are plenty of drinks, too. There might not be any real magic in the recipes, but there *is* magic in sharing a meal across a table from people you love . . . even if they do eat chili fries in your bed sometimes. Happy cooking (and hunting)!

CHAPTER 1

BREAKFAST

"Rise and shine, Sammy!"

. . . .

No meal is more important to the Winchesters than breakfast (unless we're talking about Dean and his bacon cheeseburgers . . . but according to him, that's breakfast, too). They love a classic diner breakfast of pancakes or waffles, always with black coffee and a side of bacon. Most of the recipes in this chapter are ideal for weekends—as in, they take a little while to put together—but any of them can be prepped the night before and reheated in the morning before you run out the door to your next case.

HEAVENLY PANCAKES

When Chuck returns to fight Amara in "We Happy Few," he holes up in the bunker with Sam, Dean, and a resentful Lucifer (who's inside Castiel's body). "This is the worst episode of *Full House* ever," Dean says. But at least there are pancakes, made by Chuck himself, wearing an apron, wielding a spatula, and drinking coffee from a World's Greatest Dad mug.

These pancakes aren't actually from heaven, but they *are* divine: incredibly light and fluffy, thanks to extra leavening agents that let the batter reach skyward. Once you combine everything, be sure to give the mix time to rest and work its magic before cooking.

PREP TIME:
15 minutes
COOK TIME:
15 minutes
YIELD:
12 pancakes

• **2 cups all-purpose flour**
• **¼ cup baking powder**
• **2 teaspoons baking soda**
• **1 teaspoon salt**
• **¼ cup sugar**
• **2 cups milk**
• **2 eggs, beaten**
• **¼ cup (½ stick) butter, melted**
• **2 teaspoons vanilla extract**
• **Nonstick cooking spray**
• **Maple syrup and fresh fruit for serving**

1. In a medium bowl, whisk together the flour, baking powder, baking soda, salt, and sugar.

2. In a large bowl, whisk together the milk, eggs, melted butter, and vanilla. Gradually stir the dry ingredients into the wet, being careful not to overmix. Let the batter sit 10 minutes.

3. Heat a large skillet over medium heat. Off the heat, spray the pan with nonstick cooking spray. Return the skillet to the heat and drop the batter by tablespoons into the pan, being careful not to crowd the pancakes.

4. Cook until the bottoms of the pancakes are golden brown and air bubbles are rising to the surface, about 3 minutes. Flip and cook another 2 to 3 minutes, until golden brown. Remove from the heat and transfer to a plate tented with aluminum foil to keep the pancakes warm. Repeat with the rest of the batter. Serve with maple syrup and fresh fruit.

DEAN'S BREAKFAST BACON CHEESEBURGERS WITH HONEY SRIRACHA AIOLI

The Winchester brothers, at one point or another, both feel like they're living on borrowed time. After he makes a deal with a Crossroads Demon to save Sam, Dean goes for broke, eating his beloved burgers whenever he wants. When Bobby sees Dean cooking them for breakfast, he says,

"You eating bacon cheeseburgers for breakfast now?"

"Sold my soul," Dean says. "Year to live."

You might not want to cook these burgers in the morning, but they *do* have all the components of a great breakfast: sunny-side up eggs, crispy bacon, and a spicy, sweet sauce. Feel free to swap out the bacon for sausage patties and adjust the spiciness of the Honey Sriracha Aioli to your taste. Serve with home fries and the rest of the aioli as a dipping sauce—you won't regret it.

PREP TIME:
15 minutes
COOK TIME:
15 minutes
YIELD:
4 servings

- -

HONEY SRIRACHA AIOLI
- **½ cup mayonnaise**
- **1 tablespoon sriracha**
- **1 teaspoon honey**
- **1 teaspoon lemon juice**
- **1 clove garlic, mashed**

BURGERS
- **1½ pounds ground beef**
- **1 tablespoon neutral cooking oil**
- **4 slices American cheese**
- **4 Hawaiian hamburger buns or any other large, slightly sweet rolls**
- **Salt and pepper**

TOPPINGS
- **2 tablespoons butter**
- **4 eggs**
- **8 slices cooked bacon**

1. To make the aioli: Combine the mayonnaise, sriracha, honey, lemon juice, and garlic in a glass bowl. Mix well with a fork until smooth, then cover and refrigerate while you prepare the remaining ingredients.

2. To make the hamburgers: Divide the ground beef into four equal-sized patties. Forming them loosely will ensure more even cooking. Season both sides with salt and pepper.

3. Heat the oil in a large, heavy frying pan over high heat. Cook the burgers on high, 4 minutes per side for medium and 5 minutes per side for medium-well, making sure there's a good sear on the outside. Remove from the heat, top with cheese, and tent with foil to keep warm.

4. To make the toppings: Wipe out the pan and melt 1 tablespoon of the butter over medium heat. Break the eggs one at a time and gently add them to the pan. Cook the eggs for 2 to 3 minutes, until the edges are golden brown, the whites are opaque, and the yolks have begun to set but aren't fully cooked. Remove from the heat.

5. Wipe out the pan and melt the remaining 1 tablespoon butter over medium heat. Grill the buns, cut-sides down, for about 1 minute, until golden. Remove from the heat.

6. Slather the top and bottom insides of the buns with the aioli, then layer the burger, egg, and bacon inside.

CUS'S BEST BANANA PANCAKES

When Dean brings Sam to Cus's Place in "Bad Boys," it isn't really for the food: It's to see Robin, a server there who's an old flame of Dean's. Sam offers to order burgers to go, but Dean isn't having it. "What," he says, "and miss out on the best banana pancakes you ever had?"

These banana pancakes are, hands down, the best you'll ever have. Unbelievably fluffy, banana bread—inspired pancakes are topped with cinnamon-spiced sautéed bananas and drizzled with a salted caramel sauce that's equal parts sweet and savory. The combination is otherworldly—and perfect for breakfast on a special occasion. If you want to save a step, buy premade salted caramel sauce, or substitute chocolate-hazelnut spread for a more chocolatey breakfast.

> PREP TIME:
> **15 minutes**
> COOK TIME:
> **20 minutes**
> YIELD:
> **12 pancakes**

. . . .

BANANA BREAD PANCAKES

- 1 cup all-purpose flour
- 1 teaspoon baking powder
- 1 teaspoon baking soda
- ¼ teaspoon salt
- ½ teaspoon ground cinnamon
- ¼ teaspoon ground nutmeg
- ¼ cup loosely packed light brown sugar
- 2 very ripe bananas
- 1 egg
- 2 tablespoons butter, melted, at room temperature
- 1 cup buttermilk
- 1 teaspoon vanilla extract
- ½ cup chocolate chips (optional)
- Nonstick cooking spray

SALTED CARAMEL SAUCE

- ¼ cup (½ stick) butter
- ¼ cup heavy cream
- ½ cup loosely packed light brown sugar
- ½ teaspoon coarse sea salt or more to taste
- 2 tablespoons water (optional)

SAUTÉED BANANAS

- 1 tablespoon butter
- 2 medium-ripe bananas, sliced into rounds
- ½ cup sliced strawberries or blueberries (optional)
- 1 teaspoon ground cinnamon

1. To make the banana bread pancakes: Whisk together the flour, baking powder, baking soda, salt, cinnamon, nutmeg, and brown sugar in a large bowl. In another bowl, mash the bananas and add the egg, melted butter, buttermilk, and vanilla. Make sure the melted butter isn't too hot or it will curdle the cold dairy products.

2. Stir the wet ingredients into the dry ingredients, being careful not to overmix. Let the batter rest for 5 minutes.

3. Heat a large skillet over medium heat. Off the heat, spray the pan with nonstick cooking spray. Return the pan to the heat and drop the batter by tablespoons into the pan, being careful not to crowd the pancakes. If using chocolate chips, sprinkle a few on the top of the wet batter when you add it to the pan. Cook until the bottoms of the pancakes are golden brown and air bubbles are rising to the surface, about 2 minutes, then flip and cook for 1 to 2 minutes more until golden brown. Transfer the cooked pancakes to a plate and tent them with foil to keep warm until ready to serve. Repeat with the remaining batter.

4. To make the salted caramel sauce: In a medium saucepan, combine the butter, cream, and sugar. Heat over medium-high until the sugar is melted, then reduce the heat to a simmer.

5. Cook for 5 minutes, stirring often. You want the caramel to be golden brown but not burned, so keep a close eye on it as the color starts to change.

6. Remove the caramel from the heat and add salt to taste. The sauce will thicken as it cools; add 1 or 2 tablespoons of water to thin it out into more of a maple syrup consistency, or omit if you prefer a thicker sauce.

7. To make the sautéed bananas: Melt the butter in a small skillet over medium heat. Add the bananas and berries (if using), sprinkle with cinnamon, and cook. Stir until soft, 2 to 3 minutes.

8. To serve, make a stack of pancakes, top with fruit and drizzle with sauce.

ANGEL EGG WHITE OMELET

After Sam restores Dean's humanity, Dean struggles to live with the Mark of Cain without going dark again. He takes on a "twelve-step program not to backslide" that involves good sleep, no booze, and a clean diet—like these egg white omelets he makes for breakfast. "Breakfast of champions . . . you know, if you're a dork like you," Dean says. "Wow, that's awesome," Sam replies. "It's crap," Dean says. "As soon as I get rid of this demonic tramp stamp, I'm back on booze, burgers, and more booze."

Sam's right, though—this omelet is full of flavor and low on fat. Feel free to get creative with the fillings. The recipe calls for onion, spinach, and tomato, but avocado, mushrooms, or broccoli would all work well, too. Small amounts of feta or goat cheese offer a lot of flavor, but you could get the same result with Parmesan or aged cheddar, too. Serve with more spinach or whole wheat toast.

PREP TIME:
5 minutes

COOK TIME:
10 minutes

YIELD:
4 servings

- **Nonstick cooking spray**
- **1 small yellow onion, chopped**
- **2 small tomatoes, chopped**
- **1 cup fresh baby spinach**
- **12 egg whites, divided**
- **¼ cup crumbled feta or goat cheese, divided**
- **Salt and pepper**

1. Heat a medium skillet over medium-high heat. Off the heat, spray the pan with nonstick cooking spray. Return the pan to the heat, add the onion and cook, stirring, for 3 minutes, then add tomatoes and cook, stirring often, another 3 minutes, until soft. Add the spinach and cook 2 more minutes, until slightly wilted. Remove from the heat and cover to keep warm.

2. Heat a small skillet over medium heat. Off the heat, spray the pan with nonstick cooking spray. Return the pan to the heat, add 3 of the egg whites, and cook until they start to turn opaque, about 3 minutes. Season to taste with salt and pepper, and add a quarter of the vegetables and cheese. Fold over and transfer to a plate.

3. Repeat with the remaining eggs, vegetables, and cheese.

MONSTER FOODS

The Winchesters may be saving the world, but they also save countless people from becoming dinner. Different monsters live off of different parts of humans. Wraiths, as seen in episodes like "Sam, Interrupted," use long spikes to feed off human brains. Changelings feed off human synovial fluid, like in "The Kids Are Alright." In "Ourobouros," a gorgon eats human eyes to see into the future. Kitsune, in "The Girl Next Door," feast on pituitary glands. Pishtaco, in "The Purge," eat only fat. Werewolves, in episodes like "Monster Movie," eat human hearts. Some creatures, like the Wendigo, want to eat everything. So . . . hungry yet?

PIG 'N A POKE

"Hey, Tuesday!" Dean says, looking at the wall of specials in the diner: "Pig 'n a Poke." He orders it with a side of bacon and coffee, and then orders it again and again, as he and Sam repeat the same day. While Dean eats and eats, Sam tries to break the Trickster's cycle and find a way to rescue his brother from getting killed over and over in the time loop.

This twist on Dean's "Mystery Spot" breakfast takes the side of bacon and incorporates it into the main event: sausages, wrapped in pancakes, then wrapped in bacon. Top them with good maple syrup for the ultimate sweet and savory breakfast combination—no mystery about it.

PREP TIME:
10 minutes
COOK TIME:
10 minutes
YIELD:
4 servings

• •

- **8 Heavenly Pancakes (page 11)**
- **8 breakfast sausage links**
- **8 slices bacon**
- **Maple syrup for serving**

1. Prepare the pancakes according to the recipe directions, and tent with aluminum foil to keep warm.

2. Brown the sausages and bacon over medium heat in a large skillet, making sure the bacon is still flexible and isn't too crispy. Remove from the heat and drain on a paper towel.

3. Wrap a sausage in a pancake, then wrap the pancake in a slice of bacon. Secure with a toothpick. Serve with maple syrup.

METATRON'S WAFFLES

When Metatron is leading Castiel on a wild goose chase to recover his grace in "Book of the Damned," the two stop at a diner for Metatron's first-ever meal as a human. The waffles he orders exceed his every expectation. "O. M. Me," Metatron says. "Food, glorious food. All the countless descriptions in so many books, but those are just words. The taste! The actual taste . . . I had no idea."

Spoiler alert: You're probably going to have the same reaction when you try these transcendent strawberry-vanilla waffles. The waffles themselves have a delicate vanilla scent and are filled with fruit, but then, they're topped with a fresh, not-too-sweet strawberry sauce that's just begging for whipped cream. Serve these for breakfast or add some vanilla ice cream and enjoy them as strawberry-vanilla waffle sundaes for dessert. They're that good.

PREP TIME:
15 minutes
COOK TIME:
30 minutes
YIELD:
8 waffles

. . . .

STRAWBERRY SAUCE
- **1 pound strawberries**
- **½ cup sugar**
- **Juice of ½ lemon**

WAFFLES
- **2 cups all-purpose flour**
- **½ cup sugar**
- **4 teaspoons baking powder**
- **¼ teaspoon salt**
- **2 eggs, divided**
- **1¾ cups milk**
- **½ cup (1 stick) butter, melted and cooled**
- **2 teaspoons vanilla extract**
- **1 cup strawberries, chopped**
- **Nonstick cooking spray**
- **Whipped cream or ice cream for serving (optional)**

1. To make the strawberry sauce: Chop the strawberries, discarding the stems and hulls. Combine them with the sugar and lemon juice in a medium saucepan. Bring to a boil over medium heat, then reduce to a simmer and cook for about 15 minutes, until the fruit has mostly broken down and the sauce has thickened. Remove from the heat and set aside to cool.

2. To make the waffles: In a medium bowl, whisk together the flour, sugar, baking powder, and salt. In a large bowl, whisk together the egg yolks, milk, butter, and vanilla. Add the dry ingredients to the wet, whisking well to combine.

3. In the bowl of a mixer fitted with a balloon whip, whip the egg whites on medium-high speed until glossy peaks form.

4. Fold the egg whites into the batter, and then gently add the chopped strawberries. You want this batter to be light as air, so be careful not to overmix when adding the final ingredients.

5. Spray a waffle iron with nonstick cooking spray and add ½ cup of batter to the iron. Cook according to the waffle iron's directions, until golden brown. Transfer each waffle to a plate tented with aluminum foil to keep warm until you're ready to serve. Top with strawberry sauce, and whipped cream or ice cream if using, and enjoy.

WALDO'S WAFFLES

When Dean wakes up in a park in Eureka Springs, Arkansas, in "Regarding Dean," he has no idea where he is or why he's there. He does, though, know what he wants for breakfast. "I'm starving. How do you feel about waffles?" Dean asks when he calls Sam to get picked up.

"Dumb question. Right.
What psycho doesn't love waffles?"

When Sam arrives at Waldo's Waffles, Dean has demolished one plate of waffles and orders a second. "Maybe let's pump the brakes a little bit," Sam says. "You're not 20 anymore." "Number one, the Rat Pack partied until the day they died, and two, I can still kick your ass," Dean replies, before shouting another order of waffles for his brother.

These savory waffles are so delicious that you'll want to order two plates of them—and the good news is that these bacon, cheddar, and scallion beauties are versatile enough to have for breakfast (try them topped with over-easy eggs) or for dinner as a side dish. The best way to eat them, though? In place of bread on a sandwich. Try them with leftover Beer Chicken (page 81) and some melted brie. You won't regret it.

PREP TIME:
10 minutes
COOK TIME:
30 minutes
YIELD:
8 waffles

. . . .

- 1 cup all-purpose flour
- ½ cup cornmeal
- ¼ cup cornstarch
- 1 teaspoon baking powder
- 1 teaspoon baking soda
- 2 teaspoons salt
- ½ teaspoon pepper
- 1 teaspoon onion powder
- 1½ cups milk
- 3 eggs, beaten
- ¼ cup (½ stick) butter, melted and cooled
- ½ cup shredded cheddar cheese
- ¼ cup chopped scallions, both white and green parts
- 4 slices cooked bacon, crumbled
- Nonstick cooking spray
- Butter and maple syrup for serving

1. In a medium bowl, whisk together the flour, cornmeal, cornstarch, baking powder, baking soda, salt, pepper, and onion powder.

2. In a large bowl, whisk together the milk, eggs, and butter, mixing thoroughly. Add the dry ingredients to the wet, stirring to combine, just enough to get rid of large lumps.

3. Stir in the cheese, scallions, and bacon.

4. Spray a waffle iron with nonstick cooking spray, and spoon ½ cup of batter into the iron. Cook, according to the waffle iron directions, until golden brown. Transfer to a plate tented with foil to keep warm while you cook the rest of the waffles. If they soften too much, you can warm the waffles in a 200°F oven on a baking sheet while you cook the rest.

A BROTHER'S LOVE (of Lucky Charms)

Food is often a source of contention between the boys (mainly Sam chastising Dean for his unhealthy eating habits and Dean teasing him back for his salad-eating ways) but can also be a source of familial love and comfort. In "Something Wicked This Way Comes," Sam and Dean track down a monster that John Winchester has faced before. Dean also faces some demons from his past, like tough memories of a childhood where his dad wasn't around very much. He thinks back to a time when he had to take care of Sam, including preparing dinner in their motel room. "I'm sick of Scabetti-Oh's," a young Sam complains. "You're the one who wanted 'em," Dean responds. Sam asks for Lucky Charms, and he replies that there aren't any left. "OK, maybe there is," Dean says, "but there's only enough for one bowl and I haven't had any yet." Still, his love for his brother wins out, and Dean hands him a new bowl and the cereal box. Sam reaches inside, and holds out his little hand. "Do you want the prize?"

MARK OF CAIN GREEN SMOOTHIE

Dean's commitment to clean living as a way to manage the Mark of Cain goes way beyond egg white omelets (page 17). "If Cain found a way to live with it after going dark side, then I just gotta find a way to keep it in check," he says. Dean tries to love Veggie Tofu Burgers (page 51) and Kale Pita Wraps (page 47), and even tries to drink green smoothies . . . without much success.

If you've never had green juice before, you probably aren't going to love the idea of spinach blended into a breakfast drink—but just go with it. This smoothie tastes light while still being filling, and has two or three of your five daily servings of fruits and veggies. You can use any fruits you like—just keep the sugar content low by mixing less sugary fruits like berries with higher sugar ones like bananas. Try mixing banana, strawberry, and pineapple; apple, raspberry, and orange; or blueberry and mango. The seeds add enough protein to keep you full until lunch, and the ginger gives you an awesome immuno-boost if you're feeling a little run down.

PREP TIME:
5 minutes
YIELD:
1 serving

- **2 cups leafy greens, like baby spinach or baby kale**
- **1 cup water or coconut water**
- **1 cup frozen chopped fruit**
- **1 tablespoon chia or hemp seeds**
- **1 tablespoon chopped fresh ginger (optional)**

1. In a blender, combine the greens and water or coconut water. Blend for 2 minutes, until smooth.

2. Add the fruit, chia or hemp seeds, and ginger, if using. Blend another 2 minutes. Pour into a glass and enjoy.

CHAPTER 2

APPETIZERS & ROAD SNACKS

· ·

With all the time they spend driving from case to case, Sam and Dean have gotten quite good at surviving on road snacks. The ones you'll find in this chapter are turned-up versions of what they eat. Instead of M&Ms and beef jerky, you'll find a trail mix recipe that combines the two, along with many other finger foods that the boys encounter everywhere from Hollywood movie sets to funeral receptions. Maybe you want to make them for a party, or maybe you just want to make them because they're delicious. Either way, just make them. Deliciousness awaits.

COCKTAIL WEENIES THREE WAYS

When Sam has a premonition that a man is being poisoned by car fumes in his garage in "Nightmare," he and Dean race to Michigan to try to save him—but they're too late. They know that the grieving family won't want to talk to two strangers trying to solve the case, so they pose as junior priests. "This has gotta be a new low for us," Sam says. Dean makes the most of it, though, enjoying the food put out by the family at the funeral luncheon, like cocktail weenies.

These little sausages are so easy and versatile to cook that you can do almost anything with them. Here are three suggestions: one's a little sweet, one's a little cheesy, and one doubles down on the meat by wrapping the weenies in bacon. You can't go wrong. Just don't eat them in the garage.

SWEET AND SMOKY WEENIES

PREP TIME: **1 minute**
COOK TIME: **20 minutes**
YIELD: **8 servings as an appetizer**

- ¾ cup barbecue sauce
- ¼ cup orange marmalade
- ¼ teaspoon cayenne pepper
- ¼ teaspoon ground ginger
- ½ teaspoon chili powder
- ½ teaspoon dry mustard
- One 14-ounce package cocktail weenies

1. Combine all ingredients except the weenies in a medium saucepan. Bring to a boil over medium heat, stirring often.

2. Add the weenies and cook for 15 minutes, until the sauce thickens and the weenies are heated through. Remove from the heat and serve.

BACON-WRAPPED WEENIES

PREP TIME: **10 minutes**
COOK TIME: **25 minutes**
YIELD: **8 servings as an appetizer**

- One 14-ounce package cocktail weenies
- 1 pound sliced bacon
- ½ cup loosely packed dark brown sugar

1. Preheat the oven to 400°F. Line a baking sheet with foil.

2. Cut the bacon strips into thirds. Wrap one piece of bacon around each weenie, and place seam-side down on the prepared baking sheet.

3. Sprinkle with the brown sugar.

4. Bake until the bacon is crispy and brown, about 25 minutes. Serve hot.

CHEESY WEENIES IN A BLANKET

PREP TIME: **10 minutes**
COOK TIME: **12 minutes**
YIELD: **8 servings as an appetizer**

- One 12-ounce can crescent rolls
- 8 slices American cheese
- One 14-ounce package cocktail weenies

1. Preheat the oven to 375°F. Line a baking sheet with foil.

2. Unroll the crescent rolls and cut each triangle into 3 smaller triangles.

3. Cut each slice of cheese lengthwise into 4 pieces.

4. Roll a piece of cheese around each weenie, and then roll a piece of crescent roll around the cheese, making sure to completely cover the cheese with the dough. Place seam-side down on the prepared baking sheet.

5. Bake until dough is golden brown, about 12 minutes. Serve hot.

WENDIGO-HUNTING TRAIL MIX

When Sam and Dean head out to Blackwater Ridge to search for their father in "Wendigo," they pose as rangers to team up with a sister and brother who are looking for their missing sibling. But the sister doesn't buy it, saying they didn't even bring provisions. "What do you mean we didn't bring provisions?" Dean asks, whipping out a giant bag of Peanut M&Ms. That candy comes in useful: When he's captured by the wendigo, Dean leaves a trail of them to help Sam find him. "It's better than breadcrumbs," Sam says.

This trail mix is *definitely* better than breadcrumbs. The sweet, spicy, and salty mix uses dried fruit and nuts, with a kick from wasabi peas and some extra Winchester-ness from beef jerky. Make your own perfect combination with any fruit, nuts, or salty snacks you like—just don't skip the candy.

> PREP TIME:
> **5 minutes**
> YIELD:
> **3½ cups**

• •

- ½ cup chopped beef jerky
- ½ cup Peanut M&Ms or chocolate-covered peanuts
- ½ cup wasabi peas
- ½ cup banana chips
- ½ cup dried cranberries
- ½ cup dry-roasted almonds
- ½ cup toasted pumpkin seeds

1. Combine all ingredients in a large glass jar.
2. Store in the refrigerator for up to 2 weeks (not that it will last that long).

FRIED PICKLE CHIPS WITH HOMEMADE RANCH DRESSING

After Castiel takes on all the souls of purgatory to defeat the Leviathans, he's drunk on the power. Sam, Dean, and Bobby try to bind Death to remove all those souls and restore order to Castiel (and the world). It doesn't work. "Try to bind me again, and you'll die before you start," Death says in "Meet the New Boss" as he walks away.

"Nice pickle chips, by the way."

These salty, savory pickle chips are deep-fried, and brought to a whole new level with the addition of homemade ranch dressing for dipping. You could just buy the regular stuff, but this one comes together so quickly (and with all pronounceable ingredients) that you might never go back to the bottle again.

PREP TIME:
10 minutes

COOK TIME:
20 minutes

YIELD:
8 servings as an appetizer

• •

RANCH DRESSING

- ½ cup mayonnaise
- ½ cup sour cream
- ½ cup milk
- 1 tablespoon minced fresh dill or 1 teaspoon dried dill
- 1 tablespoon minced fresh parsley or 1 teaspoon dried parsley
- 1 tablespoon minced fresh chives or 1 teaspoon dried chives
- 1 teaspoon garlic powder
- ½ teaspoon onion powder
- ½ teaspoon salt
- ¼ teaspoon pepper
- Juice of 1 lemon

PICKLE CHIPS

- 1 cup all-purpose flour
- 1½ tablespoons garlic powder
- 1 tablespoon onion powder
- 1 tablespoon salt
- 2 teaspoons black pepper
- ½ teaspoon cayenne pepper
- One 16- or 20-ounce jar dill pickle chips
- Vegetable or canola oil for frying

1. Make the ranch dressing: Whisk all the ingredients together. Cover and refrigerate in a glass container for at least an hour to let the flavors meld.

2. Make the fried pickle chips: Combine everything except the pickles and oil in a flat, shallow bowl. Set aside.

3. Drain the pickles, and pat dry with a paper towel.

4. Heat 1 inch of oil to 300°F in a Dutch oven or deep skillet.

5. Dredge pickles, one at a time, in the seasoning mixture. Fry in batches, being careful not to crowd the pan, for 2 to 3 minutes, until golden brown.

6. Remove to a paper towel–lined plate to drain. Serve with ranch dressing for dipping.

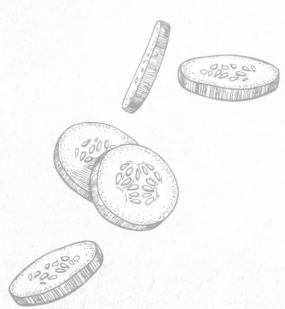

MINI PHILLY CHEESESTEAK SANDWICHES

In "Hollywood Babylon," Sam and Dean find themselves on the set of a horror film where people are actually dying. While Dean wanted to visit Los Angeles to find "swimming pools and movie stars" on a vacation, he does manage to make himself right at home during the investigation, digging into the craft services table, especially the mini Philly cheesesteaks. "Being a P.A. sucks," he says, "but the food these people get? Are you kidding me? I mean, look at these things." He's not wrong—these little versions of the classic sandwich are total crowd-pleasers. If you want to be truly authentic, go for processed cheese rather than provolone.

PREP TIME:
15 minutes
COOK TIME:
25 minutes
YIELD:
10 sandwiches

. . . .

- 2 tablespoons neutral cooking oil, divided
- 1 small yellow onion, chopped
- 1 red bell pepper, sliced
- 1 green bell pepper, sliced
- 1 cup sliced mushrooms
- 2 pounds sirloin steak, shaved or thinly sliced
- 12 slices provolone cheese
- 10 miniature sandwich rolls
- Salt and pepper

1. In a large skillet over medium-high heat, heat 1 tablespoon of the oil. Add the onion, red bell pepper, green bell pepper, and mushrooms, and cook, stirring, until caramelized, 13 to 15 minutes. Remove from the heat and transfer the vegetables to a plate.

2. In the same pan, heat the remaining 1 tablespoon oil. Season the steak with salt and pepper and cook until browned, about 5 minutes.

3. Add the vegetables back to the pan and layer the cheese over the top. Cook until the cheese is melted, about 2 minutes. Remove from the heat.

4. Divide among the sandwich rolls and serve—just not during a horror film.

SILVER SCREEN TAQUITOS

On the Hollywood set of the horror movie, Dean really embraces his role as a production assistant. "I thought you hated being a P.A.," Sam says. "I don't know," Dean replies, "it's not so bad. I kind of feel like part of the team, you know?" He then offers Sam one of the taquitos he's eating from craft services. "Taquito?" he asks Sam.

"They're wonderful."

You're going to feel the same way once you try these crunchy snacks. Serve them as an appetizer, or with rice and beans as an entree. Just maybe look out for any vengeful spirits before you sit down to eat.

PREP TIME:
5 minutes
COOK TIME:
30 minutes
YIELD:
12 taquitos

. . . .

FILLING
- **1 teaspoon onion powder**
- **1 teaspoon chili powder**
- **1 teaspoon garlic powder**
- **½ teaspoon celery salt**
- **½ teaspoon dried oregano**
- **⅛ teaspoon ground cumin**
- **⅛ teaspoon cayenne pepper**
- **¼ cup water**
- **2 cups cooked, shredded chicken**
- **1 cup shredded Monterey Jack cheese**

TAQUITOS
- **12 small tortillas**
- **¼ cup neutral cooking oil, divided**
- **1 cup shredded iceberg lettuce**
- **½ cup crumbled cotija cheese**
- **½ cup sour cream or Mexican crema**

1. To make the filling: In a medium skillet over medium heat, combine the onion powder, chili powder, garlic powder, celery salt, oregano, cumin, cayenne, and water. Add the chicken and cook until the spices have adhered well to it, 4 to 5 minutes. Remove from the heat, stir in the cheese and set aside.

2. To make the taquitos: Warm a small amount of the oil in a large skillet over medium heat and lightly fry the tortillas in a little bit of oil until just browned, about 1 minute each. Remove to paper towels to drain.

3. Divide the filling evenly among the tortillas and roll each one into a tube shape. Add the remaining oil to the large skillet over high heat, and fry the rolled taquitos in batches until crispy, 4 to 5 minutes, turning them to brown on all sides. Remove from the heat and transfer to a serving plate. Top with the lettuce, cotija, and crema to serve.

A LESSON IN CONTEMPORARY BEEF JERKY

When Mary Winchester comes back from the dead, she can't believe how much the world has changed. In "The Foundry," while they're off investigating an abandoned house, Dean introduces her to new kinds of snacks. "A lot of things have gone to seed since you were here, but the variety of snack food flavors is not one of them," he says. "You got your teriyaki jerky, you got your Sriracha, you got your chili lime, which happens to be my personal favorite." Mary is intrigued. "Let's give chili lime a whirl," she says. "It's . . . good! Artificial, kinda tingly." Dean responds, "That's how you know it's working."

BIG PRETZEL! WITH BEER CHEESE DIP

In "Monster Movie," Sam and Dean find themselves in a black-and-white movie and in search of a suspected vampire, or, as Dean says, on "an honest to goodness monster hunt." The brothers find themselves in the middle of an Oktoberfest celebration, complete with big pretzels that are so enticing to Dean that he stops mid-conversation ("Big pretzel!") to go get them.

These soft, salty pretzels stop all conversation, too, but that's because people will be too busy diving into the incredible beer cheese dip that goes them. It might seem daunting to make your own from scratch, but one taste and it will be worth the work.

PREP TIME:
40 minutes
COOK TIME:
30 minutes
YIELD:
10 pretzels

. . . .

PRETZELS

- **1½ cups warm water**
- **One ¼-ounce packet instant yeast**
- **1 teaspoon salt**
- **1 tablespoon butter, melted and cooled**
- **4 cups all-purpose flour, plus more for kneading**
- **¾ cup baking soda**
- **Sea salt**

BEER CHEESE DIP

- **2 tablespoons butter**
- **3 tablespoons all-purpose flour**
- **¾ cup milk**
- **1 cup lager beer**
- **¾ teaspoon dry mustard**
- **¾ teaspoon garlic powder**
- **½ teaspoon salt**
- **¼ teaspoon cayenne pepper**
- **3 cups shredded cheddar cheese, the bolder the better**

1. Preheat the oven to 400°F.

2. To make the pretzels: Combine the warm water and yeast in a large bowl. Add the teaspoon of salt, butter, and flour. Mix to combine until the dough isn't sticky.

3. On a floured surface, knead the dough for 5 minutes. Let it rest, covered, for 10 minutes.

4. Divide the dough into 10 sections. Roll out each section into a long rope, then fold into a pretzel shape.

5. Bring a medium pot of water to a boil and add the baking soda. Boil each pretzel for about 30 seconds. Place them on a baking sheet, making sure to let them drip well first, and sprinkle with sea salt.

6. Bake for 15 to 17 minutes, until browned.

7. To make the cheese dip: Melt the butter in a medium saucepan over medium heat, then whisk in the flour to make a roux. Remove from the heat, and whisk in the milk, then the beer, dry mustard, garlic powder, salt, and cayenne pepper. Return to the heat and add the cheese. Stir frequently until cheese is melted, about 5 minutes. Remove from the heat, transfer to a bowl, and serve with the pretzels.

CHAPTER 3

SANDWICHES & BURGERS

Maybe it's all the time the Winchesters spend in diners, but there's no food they come back to more often than sandwiches—both healthy ones like a Kale Pita Wrap that Dean eats under duress and majestically unhealthy ones, like an Elvis Burger. You can just go ahead and use your imagination to envision what that might be—or better yet, skip ahead to that recipe and try it for yourself.

ELVIS BURGER

When Dean brings home dinner to the bunker in "Don't You Forget About Me," he proudly removes a giant doughnut sandwich from the bag. "That," he says, "that's the Elvis." Sam can't believe what he's seeing. "Elvis? Is that a . . ." "That's a glazed doughnut," Dean says. "Well two, actually. One topside, one on the bottom. Now, your inferior versions, they'll just take one and split it down the middle. Boom." Sam, though, isn't convinced. "Dude, I'm not going to survive hundreds of monster attacks just to get flatlined by some double doughnut monstrosity." "It's the Elvis!" Dean says. Sam responds,

"How many calories are in that thing?"

You probably aren't going to want to think too hard about the calories in this burger, which pays homage to The King by taking the components of his favorite sandwich—peanut butter, bacon, and banana—and putting them on a burger with doughnuts for buns. One bite, though, and all your worries will be gone.

PREP TIME:
10 minutes
COOK TIME:
15 minutes
YIELD:
4 servings

- **2 pounds ground beef**
- **Salt and pepper**
- **1 tablespoon neutral cooking oil**
- **½ cup peanut butter**
- **1 tablespoon butter**
- **2 bananas, sliced**
- **2 teaspoons loosely packed dark brown sugar**
- **8 slices cooked bacon**
- **8 glazed doughnuts**

1. To make the hamburgers: Divide the ground beef into four equal-sized patties. Forming them loosely will ensure more even cooking. Season both sides with salt and pepper.

2. Heat the oil in a large, heavy frying pan over high heat. Cook the burgers on high, 4 minutes per side for medium and 5 minutes per side for medium-well, making sure there's a good sear on the outside. Remove from the heat, top with peanut butter, and tent with foil to keep warm.

3. Wipe out the pan and melt the butter over medium heat. Add the sliced bananas and brown sugar, and cook, stirring, until soft, about 3 minutes. Remove from the heat.

4. Place each hamburger on a doughnut, then top each with 2 slices of bacon and some of the bananas. Top with another doughnut and serve.

CAS'S PEANUT BUTTER AND JELLY

As a human, Castiel loved peanut butter and jelly sandwiches. "I enjoyed the taste of peanut butter and grape jelly," he says. "Not jam. Jam is unsettling." When he tries to eat the sandwich as an angel, though, he says, "I can taste every molecule." "Not the sum of its parts, huh?" Sam asks. "It's overwhelming," Cas says. "It's disgusting. I miss you, PB&J."

You're going to taste every bit of this grilled peanut butter and jelly, and you're not going to regret a single bite. Warming it up with a grilled cheese technique elevates this sandwich from childhood lunchbox staple to adult pleasure. If you want, add crispy bacon or some sautéed bananas.

PREP TIME:
5 minutes
COOK TIME:
10 minutes
YIELD:
4 servings

• **8 slices bread**
• **¼ cup (½ stick) butter**
• **½ cup peanut butter**
• **¼ cup grape jelly**
• **8 slices bacon (optional)**
• **Sautéed Bananas (page 15) (optional)**

1. Butter one side of each piece of bread. Spread the peanut butter on the second side of 4 slices of bread, and the jelly on the second side of the other 4 slices. If you're adding bacon or bananas, place them on top of the peanut butter.

2. Put the sandwiches together so the butter is on the outside and the PB&J is on the inside.

3. Heat a large skillet over medium heat. Place the sandwiches in butter-side down, and cook for 4 minutes per side, until golden brown.

KALE PITA WRAP

When Dean is on his Mark of Cain clean-eating diet, he likes it exactly as much as you'd expect. That is: not at all. When he and Sam are staking out a lead to find out what Bad Charlie is up to in "There's No Place Like Home," Dean is eating a veggie wrap in the car. All he can manage to say is,

"What the hell is kale?"

But his face really says it all.

This kale pita wrap is a lot more pleasant to eat than whatever Dean was trying to make work that day. The wrap is a vegetarian take on a Greek gyro, with a cool, cucumber-based tzatziki sauce, lots of vegetables, and chickpeas for protein. If you prefer, add plant-based "chicken" or "ground beef" for an even more filling sandwich.

PREP TIME:
15 minutes
YIELD:
4 servings

· ·

TZATZIKI

- **1 English cucumber, grated and drained of excess liquid**
- **2 tablespoons fresh dill**
- **1 clove garlic, mashed**
- **2 tablespoons lemon juice**
- **½ teaspoon salt**
- **¼ teaspoon pepper**
- **1 cup plain Greek yogurt**

WRAP

- **4 whole-wheat pita wraps, pocketless preferred**
- **1 cup baby kale**
- **½ cup crumbled feta cheese**
- **1 English cucumber, sliced into rounds**
- **1 cup chickpeas**
- **Sliced banana peppers and/or kalamata olives (optional)**

1. To make the tzatziki: Combine all ingredients in a glass bowl, mixing well. Cover and refrigerate for 30 minutes to let the flavors meld.

2. To make the wraps: Spread tzatziki on the inside of the bread, then layer in kale, cheese, cucumbers, and chickpeas. Add more sauce to taste, and banana peppers and/or olives, if using, for a flavorful punch. Use the leftover tzatziki as a dipping sauce or salad dressing.

DEATH'S HOT DOG

After Sam returns from hell, he seems fine—until Dean realizes he's missing his soul and searches for ways to restore it. In "Appointment in Samarra," Dean finally seeks out Death (by literally dying, with the help of Dr. Robert) for a solution. Death's solution: a wager. If Dean can wear his ring for 24 hours, and be Death for an entire day, then Death will restore Sam's soul.

"Join me," Death says, handing Dean a hot dog. "Brought you one from a little stand in Los Angeles known for their bacon dogs." "What's with you and cheap food?" Dean asks. "I could ask you the same thing," he responds. "I thought I'd have a treat before I put the ring back on."

These hot dogs are definitely a treat, and are modeled after the most famous bacon chili dogs in Los Angeles. Luckily, you don't have to travel far to get them—just to the kitchen and back.

PREP TIME:
20 minutes
COOK TIME:
75 minutes
YIELD:
4 servings

. . . .

CHILI
- 1 tablespoon neutral cooking oil
- 1 large red onion, chopped
- 4 cloves garlic, chopped
- 3 jalapeños, seeded and chopped
- 1½ pounds ground beef
- 3 tablespoons chili powder
- 1 tablespoon chipotle powder
- 2 teaspoons ground cumin
- 1 teaspoon smoked paprika
- 1 teaspoon cayenne pepper
- One 14-ounce can chopped tomatoes
- One 14-ounce can kidney beans
- 1 cup beef broth

HOT DOGS
- ½ cup water
- 4 beef frankfurters
- 4 slices American cheese
- 4 sub rolls, sliced lengthwise
- 8 slices cooked bacon
- 1 small yellow onion, chopped
- 1 small tomato, seeded and chopped
- 1 cup prepared chili
- ¼ cup yellow mustard

1. To make the chili: In a large pot, heat the oil over medium heat. Add the onions and cook until lightly browned, about 5 minutes, then the garlic and jalapeños, and cook for 2 more minutes, until they're starting to soften. Add the beef and brown for about 5 minutes, then add the rest of the ingredients and bring to a boil. Lower the heat to a simmer and cook for about 40 minutes, until the chili has thickened and the flavors are melded. Remove from the heat.

2. To make the hot dogs: In a large skillet, heat the water over medium-high heat until just boiling. Add the hot dogs, cover, and steam for 5 minutes, turning often to brown on all sides. Remove from the heat and drain.

3. Place one slice of cheese and then one hot dog in each bun, then divide the bacon, onion, tomato, chili, and mustard evenly among them. Serve hot.

VEGGIE TOFU BURGER

When they realize in "The Monster at the End of This Book" that Chuck is writing the brothers a future that leads them to Lilith, Sam and Dean do everything they can to change their fate—doing the opposite of their normal behaviors. "We get off book," Dean says, "we never make it to the end. It's opposite day." That means no fighting monsters, no research for Sam, and no bacon cheeseburger for Dean. He reluctantly orders a veggie tofu burger and thinks it's a miracle that it tastes so good until the waitress tells him he's gotten a bacon cheeseburger by mistake.

"Tofu is amazing!"

Don't tell Dean, but these burgers are just as good as the real thing, and a lot healthier for you. If you can find them, get the refrigerated, plant-based burgers sold in the meat section of the grocery store, rather than frozen ones. That makes all the difference in this recipe tasting like a copycat hamburger. Serve with fries, using the remaining aioli for dipping sauce, or with a side salad.

PREP TIME:
10 minutes
COOK TIME:
10 minutes
YIELD:
4 servings

. . . .

GARLIC AIOLI
- **2 cloves garlic**
- **¼ teaspoon salt**
- **Pinch of black pepper**
- **½ cup mayonnaise**
- **1 tablespoon lemon juice**

BURGERS
- **Nonstick cooking spray**
- **4 plant-based meatless "hamburger" patties**
- **4 slices sharp cheddar cheese**
- **4 large whole-wheat sandwich rolls**
- **4 slices red onion**
- **2 avocados, halved, pitted, and sliced**
- **8 crunchy lettuce leaves, like romaine or iceberg**

1. To make the garlic aioli: In a food processor, pulse the garlic cloves into a paste. Add the remaining ingredients and pulse until combined. Transfer the aioli to a glass bowl, cover, and refrigerate at least 15 minutes to allow the flavors to meld.

2. To make the burgers: Spray a large skillet with nonstick cooking spray, and then heat over medium-high heat. Cook the patties for 3 minutes per side, until seared on the outside and heated to package specifications. Place cheese slices on the patties during the last minute of cooking so the cheese melts. Remove from heat and tent with foil to keep warm.

3. Wipe out the pan, spray with nonstick cooking spray, and heat over medium-high heat. Grill the buns, cut-sides down, until golden brown.

4. Slather the toasted sides of the buns with garlic aioli, then layer the patties, onion, avocado, and lettuce inside.

ITALIAN SUB WITH JALAPEÑOS

When Sam and Dean go to investigate a town where wishes are really coming true in "Wishful Thinking," the trail leads them to #1 Lucky Chins restaurant, where Dean tests out the wishing well by dropping a coin in. "What are you gonna wish for?" Sam asks. "Shh," Dean answers. "Not supposed to tell." But when a delivery guy walks into the restaurant asking if someone ordered a footlong Italian sub with jalapeños, it's pretty clear what he wanted. There are as many ways to prepare this classic sandwich as there are numbers of Lucky Chins, so if you like some deli meats more than others, use those instead. The vinaigrette, and the spicy peppers, are what make this sandwich a true Italian sub.

PREP TIME:
5 minutes
YIELD:
4 servings

- **1 loaf crusty Italian bread**
- **¼ cup red wine vinegar, divided**
- **¼ cup olive oil, divided**
- **1 tablespoon dried parsley**
- **¼ cup pickled pepperoncini**
- **¼ cup pickled jalapeños**
- **8 slices salami**
- **8 slices mortadella**
- **8 slices ham**
- **8 slices prosciutto**
- **8 slices provolone**
- **Salt and pepper**

1. Slice the loaf of bread lengthwise, leaving the halves attached. Drizzle the insides with 2 tablespoons each of the vinegar and olive oil, sprinkle with parsley, and season with salt and pepper.

2. Spread the pepperoncini and jalapeños across the bread, then layer the meats and cheeses. Drizzle the remaining 2 tablespoons each of the oil and vinegar on top.

3. Close the two halves and cut the bread into 4 sections. Serve.

MONSTERS OUT FOR BLOOD

Vampires, which make frequent appearances on the show in episodes like "Citizen Fang," are the most famous monsters who survive on human blood, but they're not the only ones. Djinn are tattooed, humanoid monsters that put people in coma-like dream states so they can feed on their human blood for long periods of time, like in "What Is and What Should Never Be." Vitala, which usually hunt in pairs like they do in "Adventures in Babysitting," paralyze their victims with venom before drinking their blood.

53

CHAPTER 4
SOUPS, SALADS, & SIDES

• •

Sam and Dean are opposites in a lot of ways. While Sam went to college, Dean was out hunting monsters. When Sam is handling the research, Dean pounds the pavement for a different kind of research. Whereas Sam likes to exercise and meditate, Dean prefers to unwind with a beer and some '80s hair metal. There's no way the brothers are more different, though, than in their food choices. For every bacon cheeseburger Dean eats, there's a salad in front of Sam. Sam's choices are an endless source of embarrassment and mockery for Dean, while Dean's choices are a wellspring of judgment and sideways glances from Sam. This chapter is devoted to (mostly) healthy choices that would make Sam proud—plus one or two indulgences that Dean would love. It's all about balance, right?

HEALTH QUAKE SALAD SHAKE

Dean doesn't just love burgers; he loves making fun of Sam for *not* eating burgers and choosing salads instead. Take, for instance, this salad. When the cashier gives Dean a hard time about ordering a Health Quake Salad Shake, he clears his throat and says, "It's . . . uh . . . it's not mine." Then when Sam is mixing in the dressing, Dean says,

"Oh, you shake it up, baby."

You'll definitely want to shake this salad. Since the dressing is at the bottom, it keeps the rest of the salad crunchy, even for a few days. Mason jar salads are easy to prep ahead and make awesome grab-and-go lunches. The beauty is that you can customize them any way you like. Just remember to put the salad dressing first, then the harder or less absorbent items, then the softer items on top so they won't get soggy. Try hummus instead of dressing, tofu instead of chicken, beans instead of chickpeas, or brown rice or cooked sweet potatoes instead of quinoa. These salads keep for up to a week in the fridge.

PREP TIME:
10 minutes
YIELD:
4 servings

• 1 cup salad dressing (try Homemade Ranch, page 33)
• 1 cup chopped cooked chicken
• 1 cup shredded carrots
• 1 cup chickpeas, drained
• 1 cup quinoa, cooked
• 1 English cucumber, chopped
• 2 cups mixed greens

1. Divide the salad dressing among the four mason jars.

2. Layer the chicken, carrots, chickpeas, quinoa, cucumber, and greens in the jars, in that order.

3. Refrigerate until you're ready to eat, then shake in the jar and pour out into a bowl.

THE PEPPERJACK TURDUCKEN SLAMMER

When Bobby, Sam, and Dean are in the Pine Barrens in New Jersey investigating a potential Jersey Devil, they use Biggerson's as their home base, comparing notes over meals. Dean orders the new, limited-time special: the Pepperjack Turducken Slammer. As soon as he bites into it, he starts acting like a different, more relaxed person. By the second sandwich, he's totally chill. "What do you think?" Sam asks Dean about the case. "I'm not that worried about it," Dean replies. "It's funny, right? I could give two shakes of a rat's ass. Is that right? Do rats shake their ass or something else?" Sam and Bobby both notice that everyone around them is eating the Turducken, and everyone is very calm. Bobby says, "There's some funky chicken in the TDK Slammer."

Once they get it back home, Dean can't understand why he's being deprived of the most delicious thing he's ever eaten. "This is stupid. The sandwich didn't do anything. I don't know what you're going to find . . . And you know what's even better? I don't care that I don't care. I just want my damn Slammer back." Sam and Bobby start questioning what the problem could be—and the sandwich starts leaking gray goo. "OK, so whatever turned Gerald Browder into a pumpkinhead, and whatever is currently turning Dean into an idiot—" "I'm right here. Right here," Dean interjects. ". . . is in the Turducken Slammer at Biggerson's. It's in the meat," Sam says. Dean responds, "If I wasn't so chilled out right now I would puke."

It turns out the Leviathans were using tainted corn syrup from SucroCorp to make humans drugged and complacent, so they would be easier to manage on the Leviathans' quest to eat all of mankind. You probably don't want to eat the Biggerson's TDK Slammer, but you can easily make your own version at home. The recipe is simple: Order a premade Turducken from your local butcher or online. Roast it according to the directions. Slice it, and serve it as a sandwich with Pepper Jack cheese, tomato, and lettuce on a bulky sandwich roll. Maybe skip the gray Leviathan goo and use mayo instead. Or, you know, just go with it. Dean seemed to be having a great time.

SIDEWINDER SOUP & SALAD COMBO

During the Jersey Devil investigation, while Dean can't get enough of that tainted Turducken Slammer, Bobby and Sam both order salads. Brandon, the waiter who brings them, has a major attitude problem. "Sidewinder Soup and Salad goes to Big Bird, TDK Slammer goes to Ken Doll, and a little Heart Smart for Creepy Uncle," Brandon says. "What is your problem?" Dean asks. "*You* are my problem," Brandon replies. "Someone's got his flair all up in a bunch," Bobby says. Sam replies, "There goes his 18 percent."

Even if you're under the influence of Leviathan food, you're going to have a hard time finding fault with this combo, which is a grown-up take on grilled cheese and tomato soup. A super-simple roasted tomato soup is topped with grilled cheese croutons and comes with a salad lightly dressed with a classic French-style vinaigrette. The only reason you'd storm out over this combo is if someone at work tried to mess with your lunch break and you weren't able to eat it.

PREP TIME:
20 minutes
COOK TIME:
70 minutes
YIELD:
4 servings

ROASTED TOMATO SOUP

- 3 pounds assorted small tomatoes
- 6 cloves garlic, peeled
- 1 medium yellow onion, peeled and sliced
- ⅓ cup olive oil
- 4 cups vegetable stock
- ¼ cup (½ stick) butter
- ½ cup fresh basil leaves
- Salt and pepper

GRILLED CHEESE CROUTONS

- 2 tablespoons butter
- 4 slices thin white bread
- 4 slices deli cheese, like American or cheddar

SALAD

- Juice of ½ lemon
- 1 tablespoon Dijon mustard
- ¼ cup extra-virgin olive oil
- ½ teaspoon sea salt
- Pepper
- 4 cups mixed greens

1. Preheat the oven to 425°F, position a rack in the top of the oven, and line a baking sheet with foil.

2. To make the soup: Core and stem the tomatoes and spread them on the prepared baking sheet with the garlic and onion. Drizzle with olive oil, and season with salt and pepper. Roast on the top rack of the oven for about 30 minutes, until caramelized.

3. Remove from the oven and transfer everything to a large saucepan. Add the vegetable stock and butter, bring to a boil, and then simmer for 25 minutes. Turn off the heat. Tear the basil leaves and add them to the pot.

4. Blend the soup, either by transferring it to a blender or food processor, or by using an immersion blender in the pot. Return to the pot and cover to keep warm.

5. To make the grilled cheese croutons: Butter one side of all of the pieces of bread, then sandwich the cheese between the unbuttered side to make two sandwiches with the butter facing out. Heat a medium skillet over medium heat and cook the grilled cheeses until golden brown, about 2-3 minutes on each side. Remove from the heat, allow to cool slightly, and cut each sandwich into eight pieces.

6. To make the salad: Combine the lemon juice, mustard, olive oil, salt, and pepper in a small bowl. Whisk to combine. Dress the greens with the vinaigrette.

7. To serve, put greens on one side of a large plate and add a bowl of soup. Garnish with grilled cheese croutons, and enjoy knowing your meal is outside the influence of the evil powers of SucroCorp.

BOBBY'S CHINESE CHICKEN GEEZER SALAD

At Biggerson's, when Dean gets his Pepperjack Turducken Slammer, Bobby isn't impressed. "Bunch of birds shoved up inside each other," he says. "Shouldn't play God like that." "Hey, don't look at me sideways from that Chinese Chicken Geezer Salad over there, OK? This is awesome," Dean says. "Like the perfect storm of your top three edible birds."

This salad only has one of those top three, but it also has sweetness from mandarin oranges and crunch from chow mein noodles. Maybe it's for geezers, and maybe it's not really from China, but there's no denying that this salad is delicious.

PREP TIME:
15 minutes
COOK TIME:
10 minutes
YIELD:
4 servings

SALAD DRESSING

- ¼ cup rice vinegar
- ¼ cup sesame oil
- 1 teaspoon soy sauce
- 1 teaspoon grated fresh ginger
- 1 clove garlic, mashed
- 1 teaspoon sesame seeds
- Salt and pepper

SALAD

- 1 tablespoon neutral cooking oil
- 2 raw boneless chicken breasts, cut into bite-size pieces
- 1 tablespoon soy sauce
- 1 tablespoon sesame oil
- Salt and pepper
- 4 cups mixed greens
- 1 cup mandarin pieces, fresh or canned and drained
- 1 cup shredded red cabbage
- 1 cup shredded carrots
- 1 cup cooked, shelled edamame
- 4 scallions, sliced, both green and white parts
- ½ cup sliced almonds for topping
- 1 cup chow mein noodles for topping

1. To make the dressing: Whisk all ingredients together in a glass bowl, seasoning with salt and pepper to taste. Set aside.

2. To make the salad: Heat the oil in a medium skillet over medium heat, and add the chicken breast pieces, soy sauce, and salt and pepper. Cook, stirring occasionally, until the chicken is completely cooked through, about 8 minutes, adding the sesame oil toward the very end. Remove from the heat and set aside.

3. In a large bowl, combine the greens, mandarin pieces, cabbage, carrots, edamame, and scallions. Toss with the salad dressing, and divide evenly among 4 bowls. Add the chicken to each salad, and top with almonds and chow mein noodles.

SAM'S COBB SALAD

The Cobb Salad is an American classic, much like Sam Winchester himself.

This is what he orders when he and Dean are trying to act opposite of their normal behaviors, to change the fate Chuck is writing for them and not die by the hand of Lilith. Dean gives up burgers, and Sam has to give up his addiction: doing research. There's so much flavor in the salad ingredients that all you need is a simple vinaigrette to dress it. Feel free to get creative with that recipe, using champagne or red wine vinegar in place of lemon juice, or in addition to it.

PREP TIME:
10 minutes
YIELD:
4 servings

DRESSING
- Juice of ½ lemon
- 1 tablespoon Dijon mustard
- ¼ cup extra-virgin olive oil
- ½ teaspoon sea salt or more to taste
- Pepper

SALAD
- 4 eggs, hard-boiled
- 8 strips cooked bacon, crumbled
- 2 medium boneless chicken breasts, cooked and chopped
- 1 head romaine lettuce, chopped
- 1 cup small tomatoes, halved
- 1 avocado, sliced
- ½ cup crumbled blue cheese

1. To make the salad dressing: Whisk the ingredients together in a small glass bowl, seasoning with pepper and additional salt to taste.

2. To make the salad: Toss the greens with the vinaigrette, then portion onto 4 plates.

3. Arrange the remaining ingredients in strips on top of the lettuce. Artful presentation is key to a Cobb salad. Serve.

BIGGERSON'S GARLIC KNOTS

In "Bad Day at Black Rock," Dean thinks it's his lucky day when he's named the One Millionth Customer at Biggerson's Family Restaurant. But, as usual, things aren't always what they seem. His prize, which he never actually gets to collect, is free food for a year, including all the garlic knots he can eat. You probably won't eat as many of these buttery, garlicky rolls as Dean could, but they're so good that you're going to want to give it a try. Serve them as an appetizer with marinara sauce for dipping, or as dinner rolls alongside any savory main dish.

PREP TIME:
10 minutes
COOK TIME:
20 minutes
YIELD:
12 to 14 knots

· **Nonstick cooking spray**
· **6 cloves garlic, minced**
· **½ cup (1 stick) butter, melted**
· **2 tablespoons chopped parsley**
· **½ teaspoon salt**
· **One 11-ounce package pizza dough**

1. Preheat the oven to 400°F and spray a baking sheet with cooking spray.

2. Combine the garlic, butter, parsley, and salt in a small bowl.

3. Roll out pizza dough into a uniform rectangle. Using a pizza cutter, slice the dough into 12 or 14 even strips that are approximately 5 inches long and 1 inch thick. Brush with half the garlic mixture. Form the individual dough pieces into knots.

4. Space out the knots on the prepared baking sheet. Bake for 10 minutes.

5. Remove the knots from the oven, and brush with the remaining garlic mixture. Bake another 6 to 8 minutes, until garlic and knots are golden brown.

DONATELLO'S CHICKEN WINGS

Call it brain food if you must, but Donatello, the prophet Sam and Dean rely on to translate the demon tablet, can't work without extra-crispy buffalo wings. They're what allow him to think clearly enough to translate, but they're also his downfall: When Donatello goes out for another bucket of wings, he's captured by Asmodeus.

   Better to skip the wing run and just make these at home. You can get extra-crispy wings by deep frying them, but in this recipe you slow cook them in the oven for a much healthier alternative. It may take a while, but they're worth the wait. The level of spice is up to you: Choose a milder or hotter sauce depending on what your taste buds can handle. Definitely make your own buffalo sauce, rather than buying one premade. It takes two minutes and is incredibly delicious.

PREP TIME:
5 minutes
COOK TIME:
75 minutes
YIELD:
24 wings

- **24 chicken wing pieces**
- **1 tablespoon salt**
- **1 teaspoon baking powder**
- **½ cup (1 stick) butter**
- **1 cup hot sauce**

1. Preheat the oven to 250°F. Line a baking sheet with aluminum foil and place a baking rack inside.

2. Wash the chicken wings, and pat dry. Place in a medium bowl and sprinkle with the salt and baking powder, making sure the wings are evenly coated.

3. Lay the chicken wings on the rack in the prepared baking sheet, making sure none of them are touching.

4. Bake for 30 minutes, then turn the oven up to 425°F and bake for another 45 minutes, until chicken is cooked through and the skin is extra crispy.

5. Remove from the oven and allow to cool slightly.

6. In a medium saucepan over medium heat, melt the butter. Stir in the hot sauce, and simmer for 3 minutes.

7. Toss the chicken wings with the hot sauce and serve.

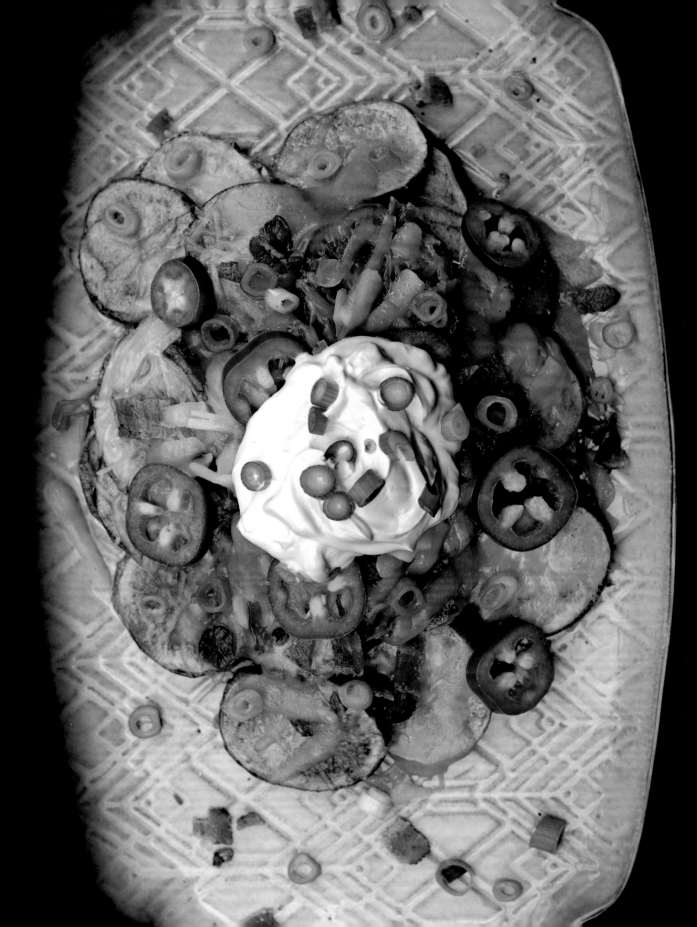

GARTH'S ROADHOUSE POTATOES

When Sam and Dean are in Missouri in "Southern Comfort" to solve the case of a woman who kills her husband over an event that happened 30 years ago, they run into Garth, who's busy in his new role organizing the hunters. The three share a meal at a roadhouse, where Garth orders a plate of potatoes and says "keep 'em coming."

You might not make it through more than one plate of these Roadhouse Potatoes, which exist at the heavenly intersection of nachos and loaded baked potatoes: Thin slices of potatoes are fried until golden, piled high and covered with cheese, bacon, jalapeños, scallions, sour cream, and more cheese. Feel free to get creative with toppings, like adding chili or shredded chicken before baking. You *could* skip making the fried potato slices and just opt for good-quality potato chips instead—but really, just make them. It's worth the extra work.

PREP TIME:
10 minutes

COOK TIME:
40 minutes

YIELD:
4 servings as an appetizer or side

• •

- **3 tablespoons butter**
- **3 tablespoons vegetable or canola oil**
- **5 to 6 russet potatoes (about 3 pounds) sliced into ¼-inch rounds**
- **Garlic salt, or salt and pepper**
- **1 cup chili or shredded chicken (optional)**
- **2 cups shredded cheddar cheese**
- **4 to 6 slices cooked bacon, chopped into small pieces**
- **4 jalapeños, seeded and sliced into rounds**
- **½ to 1 cup sour cream**
- **3 scallions, sliced, both green and white parts**

1. Preheat the oven to 350°F.

2. In a large skillet, heat the butter and oil over medium-high heat until sizzling. Fry the first round of potatoes in a single layer until golden brown but still a little bit tender, about 2-3 minutes. Remove from the pan, drain on paper towels, and repeat until all potatoes are cooked. You may need to lower the temperature if the oil becomes too hot and starts to spatter. Season to taste with garlic salt, or salt and pepper, depending on your preference.

3. Arrange the cooked potatoes in an overlapping pile, like you would with nacho chips, on an ovensafe platter or baking sheet. Top with chili or chicken, if using, then sprinkle with cheese and bacon.

4. Bake for 8 to 10 minutes, until the cheese is melted. Remove from the oven.

5. Top with jalapeños, dollops of sour cream, and scallions. Share (or don't) with friends.

"HEALTHY" BUFFALO CAULIFLOWER

Sam is always trying to get Dean to eat healthier, but unless he's under threat from some kind of demonic influence, Dean refuses to give up his burger-and-beer ways. This buffalo cauliflower, however, might make him think differently about healthy food. While it's still a vegetable, it's a yummy vegetable baked with spices and covered in spicy sauce that tastes everything like buffalo and nothing like cauliflower. Serve it as a side dish or as an appetizer with blue cheese dressing. Give it to your pickiest eaters and watch it disappear.

PREP TIME:
10 minutes

COOK TIME:
25 minutes

YIELD:
4 servings as a side or 8 servings as an appetizer

- 1 head cauliflower
- 1 cup all-purpose flour
- 1 cup water
- 1 tablespoon garlic powder
- 1 teaspoon smoked paprika
- ½ teaspoon salt
- ¼ teaspoon pepper
- 1 cup hot sauce
- 2 tablespoons butter

1. Preheat oven to 425°F. Line a baking sheet with foil.

2. Chop the cauliflower into bite-sized florets.

3. Combine the flour, water, garlic powder, smoked paprika, salt, and pepper in a bowl, and stir until smooth.

4. Dip the florets into the batter and place, one at a time, on the baking sheet, leaving space in between each one. Bake for 20 minutes.

5. In a medium saucepan over medium heat, melt the butter. Stir in the hot sauce, and simmer for 3 minutes.

6. Remove the cauliflower from the oven and brush with the hot sauce mixture. Bake about 5 more minutes, until crispy and hot.

7. Remove from the oven, allow to cool slightly, and serve.

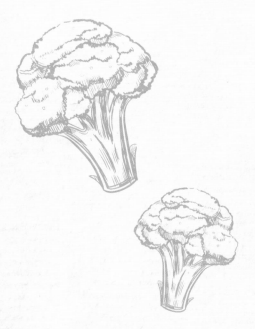

DRINKING YOUR VEGETABLES
In "Rock Never Dies," the trail to hunt Lucifer—who's currently in the body of rock star Vince Vicente—leads Sam and Dean to Los Angeles. In the lobby of Vicente's hotel, Sam pours himself a glass of cucumber-infused water. Dean is horrified. "What?" he says. "It's good." "It's *vegetable* water," Dean replies. But that doesn't stop him from trying some later. Sam can't believe it. "Seriously?" he asks. "What?" Dean responds. "Shut up." Infusing water is as simple as slicing up vegetables and fruits and adding them to a pitcher of water—but you can make the combinations as complicated as you like. Try grapefruit and fresh mint, or lemon and fresh thyme, or strawberries and basil leaves.

CHILI CHEESE FRIES

When Sam's enjoying his shaken salad at the diner, Dean's got a big plate of chili cheese fries in front of him. But that's not the only time Dean eats his favorite greasy snack. He also dives into a giant pile (on Sam's bed, no less) in "Tall Tales" while they're on the trail of the Trickster. For a slightly healthier version of these indulgent fries, try them in the air fryer or bake them in the oven instead. But really, they're chili cheese fries. Listen to the little Dean on your shoulder, ignore the Sam on your other one, and just go for it.

PREP TIME:
2½ hours
COOK TIME:
45 minutes
YIELD:
4 servings

• **2 pounds large potatoes, like russet**
• **Neutral oil for frying**
• **Salt**
• **2 cups prepared chili (page 49)**
• **2 cups shredded cheddar cheese**
• **Sour cream and sliced scallions, if desired**

1. Peel the potatoes if desired. Cut each potato into 8 or more long, thin strips. The skinnier they are, the crispier they'll be. Soak in cold water for at least 2 hours, or overnight.

2. Preheat the oven to 350°F. Drain the potatoes and dry with paper towels.

3. Heat 2 inches of oil to 300°F in a large skillet or Dutch oven. Fry the potatoes in batches until golden brown and remove to paper towels to drain.

4. Transfer the fries to an oven safe platter, then top with the chili and cheese. Bake until the cheese is melted, 8 to 10 minutes.

5. Top with sour cream and scallions, if using.

SUCROCORP GRILLED CORN WITH HERB BUTTER

SUCROCORP

The evil empire that is SucroCorp is more than just a company pumping out tainted corn syrup that turns people into brainwashed zombies. It's also a front for the Leviathans, led by Dick Roman, in their quest to take over humanity. When Sam and Dean meet Charlie Bradbury for the first time in "The Girl with the Dungeons and Dragons Tattoo," there's a SucroCorp commercial playing in the background. "America: A nation of greatness," the narrator says as someone serves himself a piece of corn on the cob. "A nation of hardworking individuals. And rest assured no one works harder for you than SucroCorp. Here at SucroCorp, your well-being is our number one priority. SucroCorp: Eat well, live well."

There are no mind-controlling substances in this recipe, unless you count the irresistible herb butter that you'll want to put on everything. The good news is that it takes almost no time to make. Use what's left on other vegetables or on bread. You can't go wrong.

PREP TIME:
10 minutes
COOK TIME:
30 minutes
YIELD:
4 servings

. . . .

HERB BUTTER
- **1 cup (2 sticks) butter, melted**
- **4 tablespoons fresh herbs, such as chives, rosemary, thyme, or parsley, chopped**

CORN
- **4 ears fresh corn, shucked**
- **Salt and pepper**

1. To make the herb butter: Combine herbs and butter in a medium bowl. Cover and refrigerate for at least an hour, until the butter is firm. If you prefer a smoother butter, combine the herbs with room temperature butter in a food processor.

2. To make the corn: Heat a grill to high heat. Wrap each individual ear of corn in foil, and grill for about 30 minutes, until corn is tender.

3. Remove from heat, allow to cool slightly and unwrap corn. Serve with herb butter, and season with salt and pepper.

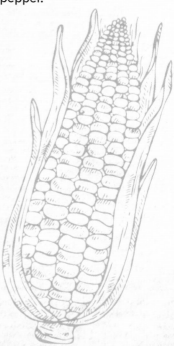

CHAPTER 5

ENTREES

· ·

Dinner is a time to gather your family around the table and take stock of your day: the good things that happened, the things you wish had gone differently, and the things you want to do better tomorrow. For Sam and Dean, though, dinner is a lot more than that. Sometimes it's what you eat from a to-go container while you're on a stakeout. Sometimes it's what you have while you're meeting with demons or fellow hunters—or both. And sometimes, in the case of a certain pizza Dean shares with Death, it's a meal that can save the world.

WINCHESTER SURPRISE

No *Supernatural* food is more legendary than Winchester Surprise, the one thing Mary Winchester cooked for her boys that she actually made herself. It's what Dean tries to make for Sam when they're kids to re-create the comfort of home, and what the four share as a family in Lebanon when John Winchester is brought back to life (if only for a little while) by a wish-granting pearl.

There's no official recipe for Winchester Surprise other than meat, cheese, and corn chips. This take on the legendary family food is a riff on a cheeseburger casserole that uses biscuits as "buns" that bubble up through the meat. Share it with people you love when you're looking for a dose of nostalgic comfort food. Whether you choose to top it with just cheese or with cheese and corn chips is up to you, but it won't *really* be Winchester Surprise without them.

PREP TIME:
15 minutes

COOK TIME:
40 minutes

YIELD:
6 servings

. . . .

- **One 12-ounce can buttermilk biscuits**
- **1 large yellow onion, diced**
- **1 pound ground beef**
- **1 pound ground pork**
- **2 tablespoons Worcestershire sauce**
- **½ cup ketchup**
- **½ cup mustard**
- **¾ cup dill pickles, chopped**
- **8 slices American cheese**
- **Corn chips for garnishing (optional)**

1. Preheat the oven to 375°F.

2. Cut each raw biscuit into 6 or 8 pieces, and scatter across the bottom of a 9-by-13-inch baking dish.

3. In a large sauté pan or skillet over medium heat, cook the onion, beef, and pork until browned, about 8 minutes. Add the Worcestershire sauce, ketchup, and mustard, and cook another 3 to 4 minutes, until the mixture thickens slightly. Remove from the heat and stir in the pickles.

4. Pour the mixture over the biscuits and top with the cheese.

5. Bake for about 35 to 40 minutes, until golden brown. In the last 5 minutes of baking, scatter crushed corn chips across the top, if using, or add them when the casserole comes out of the oven.

CHIPOTLE CHILI-CHANGA

When Sam and Dean are trying to figure out how to deal with Uriel in "Wishful Thinking," they go to a restaurant and hash it out over some shots. The waiter, though, won't let them talk in peace. "Radical! What else can I get you guys?" he asks. "I think we're good," Sam says. "Yeah? You want to try a couple of flavor bombs? Or a chipotle chili-changa?"

If only we could rewrite the course of that episode, Sam and Dean could have tried the deliciousness that is this Tex-Mex concoction. Rather than deep-frying the chimichanga, this recipe bakes it in the oven, freeing up those extra calories for all of the chili and sour cream on top. You could easily swap out the chicken for ground beef, shaved steak, or beans; the beauty of a chimichanga is that you can make it taste exactly how you want it to.

PREP TIME:
10 minutes
COOK TIME:
25 minutes
YIELD:
4 servings

- 1½ cups shredded cooked chicken
- ¾ cup salsa
- 1 teaspoon garlic powder
- 1 teaspoon ground cumin
- 1 teaspoon chili powder
- ½ teaspoon dried oregano
- 1 cup shredded cheddar cheese
- 4 large flour tortillas
- 2 tablespoons butter, melted
- 2 cups chili (page 49)
- 1 cup sour cream
- 1 cup crumbled queso fresco or cotija cheese
- 2 scallions, chopped, green and white parts, for garnishing

1. Preheat the oven to 400°F and line a baking sheet with foil.

2. In a medium bowl, combine the chicken, salsa, garlic powder, cumin, chili powder, oregano, and cheese. Distribute the filling evenly among the tortillas. Fold in two opposite sides of each tortilla, then fold in the other two sides, to make a burrito shape.

3. Lay each burrito seam-side down on the prepared baking sheet. Brush the tops of each one with melted butter.

4. Bake until golden brown, 20 to 25 minutes. Remove from the oven and place each burrito on a serving plate.

5. Top each with ½ cup of warmed chili, a drizzle of sour cream, and a sprinkle of queso fresco or cotija. Garnish with scallions.

THE WINCHESTER BEER OF CHOICE

If you're going for total authenticity with your *Supernatural* meals, and you want to drink like Sam and Dean, too, there's bad news: You can't. The Margiekugel they drink is a fake brand created for the show and named after production designer Jerry Wanek's mother.

BEER CHICKEN

If there's one thing Dean loves as much as a bacon cheeseburger, it's a cold beer. This recipe takes Dean's second favorite food and uses it in a totally different way: to flavor a roasted chicken. The rub in this recipe gives the bird a smoky, spicy flavor (and crazy-good crispy skin), while the beer keeps the meat moist and flavorful. And it's so easy that even a Winchester could cook it. Serve with vegetables, potatoes, and—what else?—a cold one.

PREP TIME:
10 minutes
COOK TIME:
90 minutes
YIELD:
4 servings

- **1 teaspoon paprika**
- **1 teaspoon dried thyme**
- **1 teaspoon black pepper**
- **½ teaspoon cayenne pepper**
- **2 teaspoons salt**
- **2 teaspoons garlic powder**
- **2 teaspoons onion powder**
- **1 whole chicken, 4 to 5 pounds**
- **One 12-ounce can lager beer**
- **1 cup chicken broth (optional)**

1. Preheat the oven to 400°F.

2. Stir together the paprika, thyme, black pepper, cayenne pepper, salt, garlic powder, and onion powder in a small bowl. Set aside.

3. Remove the neck and giblets from the chicken and discard. Wash the bird in cold water and pat dry.

4. Pour half the beer out (or into your mouth). Place the can in the middle of a roasting pan with high sides, then gently slide the chicken cavity over it so the bird is standing up. Rub the spices all over the bird.

5. Cover with foil and bake for 45 minutes. Uncover, baste with juices or chicken broth, if needed, and bake another 45 minutes, basting often, until the internal temperature of the thickest part reaches 180°F.

6. Remove the chicken from the oven and transfer it to a cutting board. Let it rest at least 10 minutes before carving.

FAT MACK'S BBQ BABY BACK RIBS

Fat Mack's Rib Shack is an important location to the Winchesters.

It's where they fuel up before hunting and where they meet Crowley when the demon threatens to send Sam back to hell, or to set him free if the brothers produce an Alpha for him.

If Dean had his way, he'd be eating the slow-cooked ribs from Fat Mack's Rib Shack every day—but that's life on the road for you. Re-create these barbecue baby back ribs at home by using a one-two punch of a spicy dry rub and smoky barbecue sauce. Rather than spending all day at the grill, though, cook them low and slow in the oven, and spend those two hours scouring the news for new cases.

PREP TIME:
5 minutes
COOK TIME:
3 hours
YIELD:
4 servings

. . . .

RUB
- **¼ cup granulated sugar**
- **¼ cup loosely packed light brown sugar**
- **2 tablespoons salt**
- **2 tablespoons black pepper**
- **1 teaspoon ground cumin**
- **1 teaspoon dry mustard**
- **1 teaspoon cayenne pepper**
- **1 teaspoon chili powder**
- **1 teaspoon garlic powder**

RIBS
- **2 racks pork baby back ribs**
- **2 cups smoky barbecue sauce**

1. To make dry rub: Combine all the ingredients in a medium bowl and mix well. Set aside.

2. Preheat the oven to 250°F.

3. To make the ribs: Wash and dry the ribs, and remove the membrane from the back with a sharp knife. (You may need to look up a video tutorial online for this.) Place the ribs individually on sheets of aluminum foil, then coat all sides with the dry rub. Wrap the ribs tightly in the foil.

4. Bake the ribs until cooked through, about 2 hours, then remove from the oven and let them sit 15 minutes to rest. Increase the oven temperature to 350°F.

5. Open the foil, drain the juices and brush the top of the ribs with barbecue sauce. Return to the oven, with the foil open, and cook 40 more minutes, brushing often with sauce.

6. Remove from the oven and allow to rest for 10 minutes. Transfer to a cutting board, cut into individual ribs, and serve.

SALT: IT'S NOT JUST FOR FOOD
Everyone's favorite tableside seasoning doesn't just make food taste better. It's also one of the things the Winchesters use to protect themselves from harm. Sam and Dean put rock salt in their shotguns to slow down menacing ghosts. They make rings of salt to keep out evil spirits and demons. They even use it to purify corpses before they burn them, to dispel the supernatural force still tied to the bones. It's best to always keep a package on hand just in case.

JODY'S CHICKEN-SHAPED ROAST CHICKEN

When Sam and Dean are visiting Jody in South Dakota in "Don't You Forget About Me," they have their first home-cooked meal in who knows how long. The brothers can't get over her simple roast chicken. "Oh, this is fantastic," Dean says. "It's just chicken," Jody replies. "It's shaped like chicken," Sam says. "Not a patty or a nugget."

This simplified version of a roast chicken is a total showstopper. It uses bone-in, cut-up pieces of chicken to give you all of the delicious roasted flavor, but cuts the cooking time in half. A simple pan sauce of wine, chicken broth, and herbs comes together in minutes. Serve it like Jody did, with mashed potatoes and green beans, and let the compliments roll in while you enjoy dinner.

PREP TIME:
5 minutes
COOK TIME:
50 minutes
YIELD:
4 to 6 servings

• •

- **6 pieces bone-in, skin-on chicken (breasts, legs, or thighs)**
- **Salt and pepper**
- **3 cloves garlic, minced**
- **½ cup dry white wine**
- **½ cup chicken broth**
- **5 tablespoons butter, divided**
- **2 tablespoons chopped fresh thyme**
- **2 tablespoons chopped fresh rosemary**

1. Preheat the oven to 425°F. Wash the chicken and pat dry. Season with salt and pepper.

2. Heat a skillet over medium-high heat and melt 2 tablespoons of the butter. Place the chicken skin-side down and sear until the skin is crispy, 5 to 6 minutes. You may need to do this in batches depending on the size of your pan.

3. Transfer the chicken to a roasting pan. Bake for 30 to 40 minutes depending on the size of your chicken pieces, until the internal temperature in the thickest part reads 180°F.

4. While the chicken is roasting, make a sauce in the skillet. Pour off most of the rendered fat but leave the brown bits in the pan. Over medium heat, brown the garlic, then add the wine and reduce for 2 to 3 minutes.

5. Add the chicken broth and cook another 3 minutes. Add the remaining 3 tablespoons butter and the thyme and rosemary, and stir until the butter is melted. Season with salt and pepper to taste.

6. Remove the chicken from the oven and allow it to rest for at least 5 minutes. Pour the sauce over the chicken and serve.

TO-DIE-FOR CHICAGO PIZZA

When the Winchesters are gathering the rings of the Four Horsemen, which together form the key to Lucifer's cage, there are serious dangers plaguing the world: disease, destruction, and Death, whom Dean finally finds at a pizzeria in Chicago, where he's about to destroy the city. "Join me, Dean," Death says. "The pizza's delicious." Death then explains that he'll loan Dean his ring as long as he's willing to let Sam jump into the cage to lure Lucifer inside. "What about Chicago?" Dean asks. "I suppose it can stay," Death says.

"I like the pizza."

This pizza might not hold the power to save the city, but it will bring down the house. Get as creative as you want to with the toppings—you could layer cooked spinach or other vegetables, or sausage or bacon (or both!) over the cheese. Don't skimp on the amount of sauce—it makes all the difference with this pie. If you're looking to save time, store-bought sauce will work just fine.

PREP TIME: **1 hour**

COOK TIME: **30 minutes**

YIELD: **4 to 6 servings**

TOMATO SAUCE

- 2 tablespoons olive oil
- 1 small onion, minced
- 4 cloves garlic, minced
- 1 teaspoon salt
- 1 teaspoon Italian seasoning
- ½ teaspoon red pepper flakes
- One 28-ounce can crushed San Marzano tomatoes

PIZZA

- One 11-ounce package raw pizza dough, at room temperature
- 2 teaspoons cornmeal
- 2 cups shredded mozzarella cheese
- ¾ cup sliced pepperoni
- 2 tablespoons grated Parmesan cheese
- Olive oil for brushing

1. To make the tomato sauce: Heat the oil in a large saucepan over medium heat, add the onion, and cook, stirring, until translucent, about 5 minutes. Add the garlic, salt, Italian seasoning, and red pepper flakes, and cook another 3 minutes. Add the tomatoes, and simmer at least 30 minutes to allow the flavors to develop. The longer you cook it, up to an hour, the better it will taste. Even better: Make it a day in advance.

2. Preheat the oven to 425°F.

3. To make the pizza: On a lightly floured surface, roll the dough out into a 12-inch circle, making sure it's a uniform thickness all around.

4. Sprinkle the cornmeal in the bottom of a 9-inch springform pan or cake pan.

5. Lay the dough over the top of the pan. Press the dough into the bottom, corners, and sides. Trim off any excess.

6. Layer the mozzarella on the bottom of the pan, followed by the pepperoni, and then top with pizza sauce. Use about a cup, or more if you like a saucy pizza. Sprinkle the Parmesan on top.

7. Brush the edges of the dough with olive oil. Bake for about 30 minutes, until golden brown. Allow to cool slightly, then slice and serve.

MARY'S PIGGLY WIGGLY MEATLOAF

Mary Winchester wasn't exactly a traditional mother to Sam and Dean growing up, but the boys did have a few happy memories of sharing home-cooked meals with her. That is, until they found out that her signature meatloaf came from the local grocery store. Moist and flavorful, this is the kind of meatloaf that's so good you'll want to make it over and over again. The mushroom gravy isn't strictly necessary, but it's worth the extra work. The best part is that there won't be any grocery store packaging to hide.

PREP TIME:
20 minutes
COOK TIME:
80 minutes
YIELD:
6 servings

MEATLOAF

- **Nonstick cooking spray**
- **1 pound ground beef**
- **1 pound ground pork**
- **¼ cup grated onion**
- **1 egg**
- **1 cup seasoned breadcrumbs**
- **¼ cup tomato paste**
- **1 tablespoon Worcestershire sauce**
- **1 teaspoon salt**
- **½ teaspoon pepper**
- **1 teaspoon Italian seasoning**
- **1 teaspoon garlic powder**

GRAVY

- **2 tablespoons butter**
- **1 pound mushrooms, cleaned and sliced**
- **2 tablespoons all-purpose flour**
- **1 teaspoon cornstarch**
- **2 cups beef stock**
- **1 teaspoon soy sauce**
- **1 teaspoon dried thyme**
- **1 teaspoon Worcestershire sauce**
- **Salt and pepper**

1. Preheat the oven to 350°F. Spray a 9-by-5-inch loaf pan with cooking spray.

2. To make the meatloaf: In a large bowl, combine all the ingredients until well mixed. Transfer to the prepared loaf pan and bake for 75 to 80 minutes, until the internal temperature reads 155°F.

3. To make the gravy: Heat a medium skillet over medium heat and melt the butter. Add the mushrooms and cook, stirring, until lightly browned, about 5 minutes. Add the flour and cornstarch, then stir until totally combined. Add the beef stock, soy sauce, thyme, and Worcestershire, and simmer about 10 minutes, until gravy is thickened. Season with salt and pepper to taste.

4. Remove the meatloaf from the oven. Allow to cool slightly, and transfer to a cutting board. Slice, top with gravy, and serve.

DEATH'S ENCHILADAS

When he summons Death to Juanita's, an abandoned restaurant in the middle of nowhere, Dean is desperate for his help to remove the Mark of Cain and makes an enormous spread of Mexican food to pique his interest. "Don't tell me that's queso," Death says. "Yes," Dean says, "queso and taquitos and tamales, handmade by yours truly. All the bad fat. Consider it an offering."

They make a big impression with Death, but these enchiladas will give you life. The bright, not-too-spicy salsa verde is a perfect choice for those who don't love spicy food, but feel free to swap out spicier red salsa (or add more jalapeños) for more of a kick. Frying the tortillas before filling makes them more pliable and easier to work with—plus, they're just more delicious that way.

PREP TIME:
20 minutes
COOK TIME:
20 minutes
YIELD:
4 servings

. . . .

- 3 tablespoons neutral cooking oil
- 8 corn tortillas
- 1 medium onion, chopped
- 4 jalapeños, seeded and diced
- 2 cups shredded cooked chicken
- 1 cup crumbled queso fresco or mild shredded cheese
- One 10-ounce can green enchilada sauce
- 1 cup crumbled cotija cheese
- 1 cup salsa verde for serving

1. Preheat the oven to 350°F.

2. In a medium sauté pan or skillet over medium-high heat, heat a small amount of the 3 tablespoons of oil. Fry the tortillas, one at a time, until lightly golden brown, about 15 seconds per side. Transfer to paper towels to drain.

3. In the same pan over medium heat, cook and stir the onions and jalapeños until soft, about 5 minutes, adding a touch more oil if necessary. Add the chicken, stir to combine and cook another 2 minutes. Remove from the heat and stir in queso fresco or other shredded cheese.

4. Divide the filling evenly among the tortillas and roll them into long cylinders. Place each one, seam-side down, into a 9-by-13-inch baking dish. Cover the enchiladas with the enchilada sauce, and top with the cotija.

5. Bake until golden brown, 15 to 20 minutes. Remove from the oven and serve with salsa verde.

CHAPTER 6

DESSERT

Being a hunter—especially one of the two most famous hunters—means making peace with not having a regular life with normal family traditions. One thing that Dean always wishes he had, and rarely manages to get, is dessert. This is especially true when it comes to pie. He orders it, and either the restaurant has run out or he has to run to chase a monster or it's baked by a zombie or the pie is cursed. This chapter is full of sweet endings to a meal. Some of them may not have gone so well on the show, but with a little bit of patience, you'll be able to remove any hexes, beating hearts, or other bad juju and just be able to enjoy them.

BUILD YOUR OWN PIE BAR

Ever the example of overeating to your heart's content (or distress), Biggerson's offers their customers a Create Your Own Pie Bar. "It's like a salad bar," they say, "but with pie!" While you could achieve a "pie bar" by just baking and setting out several pies, you can also get creative at your next dinner party. Set out small discs of pie dough, assorted fruits and fillings, sugar, and spices like cinnamon, ginger, apple pie spice, or nutmeg. Let each guest make their own individual free-form tart, then brush with an egg wash and bake at 375°F until golden brown, 35 to 40 minutes.

DIY PIE CRUST

While it's easy to buy pre-made pie crusts from the store, and they often work just as well in recipes, there's something about homemade pie crust that can't be beat. It's also surprisingly easy to make. For two crusts, which is what you'll need for one pie recipe in this chapter, add 2½ cups flour, 1 teaspoon sugar, and 1 teaspoon salt to a food processor. Pulse to combine, and then add 1¼ cups (2½ sticks) cold butter that has been cut into chunks. Mix in the food processor until the mixture is in lumps the size of peas. Continue to mix while adding ice water a tablespoon at a time— you'll need somewhere between 4 and 8 (¼ cup to ½ cup)—until the dough has combined but isn't too wet. Remove from the mixer, divide into two, wrap in plastic, and refrigerate the dough for at least 30 minutes. When you're ready, roll each half into a 12-inch disc on a floured surface, then transfer one to a 9-inch pie plate, fill, and place the other disc on top.

INGREDIENTS: Blah Blah Blah Blah Blah Blah Blah Blah Blah Blah Blah Blah Blah Blah Blah Blah Blah Blah Blah Blah Blah Blah Blah Blah Blah Blah Blah Blah Blah Blah.

I read the word "Pie."
Everything else is blah blah blah.

SUPERNATURAL
JOIN THE HUNT

MARCY'S FAMOUS GINGER PEACH COBBLER

When Marcy knocks on Bobby's door in "Weekend at Bobby's" with her baking dish in hand, she's determined to make the introduction that he never did. "Don't you think it's time you welcomed me to the neighborhood?" she asks, holding out the dessert.

"My famous ginger peach cobbler. Take a whiff. Seriously, I'm a genius."

You *could* tell people how great you are when you serve them this sweet and spicy dessert, or you could just let them take one bite and find out for themselves. Serve with ice cream or whipped cream and they'll be tossing around the compliments in no time.

PREP TIME:
20 minutes
COOK TIME:
40 minutes
YIELD:
10 to 12 servings

• •

COBBLER

- 8 peaches, peeled, pitted, and sliced (about 5 cups)
- ¼ cup granulated sugar
- ¼ cup loosely packed light brown sugar
- ½ teaspoon ground cinnamon
- ½ teaspoon ground ginger
- ¼ teaspoon ground nutmeg
- 2 teaspoons cornstarch

TOPPING

- 1 cup all-purpose flour
- ¼ cup granulated sugar
- ¼ cup loosely packed light brown sugar
- 1 teaspoon baking powder
- ½ teaspoon salt
- ½ teaspoon ground cinnamon
- ½ teaspoon ground ginger
- ½ cup (1 stick) butter, cut into small pieces
- ½ cup hot water

1. Preheat the oven to 400°F.

2. Make the cobbler: Combine all the ingredients in a large bowl and stir well with your hands, making sure all the fruit is coated with the spices and sugar. Transfer to a 9-by-13-inch baking pan.

3. Make the topping: Combine the flour, granulated sugar, loosely packed light brown sugar, baking powder, salt, cinnamon, and ginger in a medium bowl, then add the butter. Using your hands or a pastry cutter, work the butter into the mixture until it's a crumb-like texture. Add the hot water and mix to combine. Drop by spoonfuls over the fruit.

4. Bake for 35 to 40 minutes, until the topping is golden brown and the fruit is bubbling up from underneath.

SCARECROW APPLE PIE

As much as Dean is trying to live the "apple pie life" he's always talking about, he very rarely gets to eat pie when he orders it. Take the signature pie from Scotty's Cafe in Burkittsville, Indiana, where they're famous for their apples—and the town uses them as a lure to bring in outsiders as sacrifices to the Scarecrow in the crops. Dean orders a slice of the pie, doesn't get to eat it, and gets trapped by the townspeople instead. "I hope your apple pie is freakin' worth it!" he yells to the crowd. This apple pie definitely is. The secret to a perfect filling is to sauté the apples, then pour the cooled mixture into the crust before baking. Serve it at harvest time or any time—just not near any scarecrows.

PREP TIME:
40 minutes
COOK TIME:
40 minutes
YIELD:
8 servings

• **2 prepared pie crusts**
• **2 tablespoons butter**
• **5 pounds assorted apples, peeled, cored, and sliced ¼ inch thick**
• **½ cup plus 1 tablespoon sugar, divided**
• **1 teaspoon ground cinnamon**
• **½ teaspoon ground nutmeg**
• **1 tablespoon cornstarch**
• **3 tablespoons apple cider**
• **1 tablespoon lemon juice**
• **1 egg, beaten**
• **1 tablespoon milk**
• **Vanilla ice cream or Salted Caramel Sauce (page 15) for serving**

1. Preheat the oven to 375°F.

2. Melt the butter over medium heat in a heavy sauté pan or Dutch oven. Add the apples, ½ cup of the sugar, and the cinnamon and nutmeg, and sauté for 5 minutes, stirring occasionally, until the apples start to soften. Sprinkle the cornstarch over the mixture, stir, and add the apple cider. Sauté another 5 minutes, until the apples are soft but not mushy. Remove from the heat and allow to cool. Stir in the lemon juice.

3. Lay one of the pie crusts in a 9-inch pie pan, making sure the dough lays flat to the bottom and sides. Pour in the fruit mixture, then lay the other pie dough on top, firmly crimping the edges together with your fingers or a fork. Cut vents into the dough, or if you prefer, cut the top crust into a lattice pattern or other decorative shape.

4. Combine the egg and milk in a small bowl. Brush the top crust with the mixture, then sprinkle with the remaining 1 tablespoon sugar.

5. Bake for about 40 minutes, or until the crust is golden brown. Allow to cool slightly, then serve with vanilla ice cream or Salted Caramel Sauce.

BOBBY'S BOOZY BALLS

You might say Bobby likes his whiskey—or "hunter's helper," as he's been known to call it. He uses it to test for demons, offering people a drink of holy water–laced whiskey when they enter his house, and to commemorate any happy or sad occasion. He's so fond of the stuff that after Dick Roman kills him, Bobby's ghost stays on earth, attached to the hip flask he always carried. In honor of Sam and Dean's beloved mentor, this recipe combines two of Bobby's favorite things: drinking bourbon and exasperatedly exclaiming, "Balls!"

While Bobby once told Crowley he'd been drinking "rotgut aged three days," these boozy no-bake treats probably won't last that long in your house. They should sit overnight, though, to let the bourbon flavor really take hold in the chocolate. Serve them with strong coffee—with a splash more whiskey, if you'd like—for dessert or a sweet bite any time.

PREP TIME:
30 minutes
YIELD:
About 24 balls

. . . .

- **3 cups crushed vanilla wafers**
- **1 cup ground almonds**
- **¼ cup honey**
- **2 cups confectioners' sugar, divided**
- **½ cup bourbon**
- **6 tablespoons dark chocolate cocoa powder, divided**

1. Combine the crushed cookies, ground almonds, honey, 1 cup of the confectioners' sugar, bourbon, and 5 tablespoons of the cocoa powder in a large bowl. Stir well. Refrigerate for 10 minutes.

2. Combine the remaining 1 cup sugar and 1 tablespoon cocoa powder in a shallow bowl. Set aside.

3. Roll the dough into 1-inch balls, then drop individually into the sugar mixture to coat. Set on a platter or in small baking cups. Refrigerate overnight to let the flavors develop—if you can wait that long. The balls will keep for a few days in the refrigerator.

BEATING HEART CUPCAKES

When Don Stark's wife, Maggie, is angry about his infidelities, she takes it out on the whole town, including hexing his assistant, Wendy. She takes a bite of a pretty cupcake and finds a beating heart inside—and narrowly escapes a gruesome fate. "There were hearts in my cupcakes," she says.

"Hearts in my cupcakes! That's never happened before."

The "hearts" of raspberry preserves in these vanilla-raspberry cupcakes are more delicious than terrifying. Still, you might want to check for hexed coins in your kitchen before you enjoy them.

PREP TIME:
30 minutes
COOK TIME:
20 minutes
YIELD:
12 cupcakes

. . . .

VANILLA-RASPBERRY CUPCAKES

- 2 eggs
- 1 cup granulated sugar
- 1 cup (2 sticks) butter, at room temperature
- 1 tablespoon vanilla extract
- 2 cups all-purpose flour
- ¾ cup milk
- 2 teaspoons baking powder
- ½ teaspoon salt
- 1 cup seedless raspberry preserves

RASPBERRY BUTTERCREAM

- ½ cup butter, at room temperature
- 4 cups confectioners' sugar
- 1 teaspoon vanilla extract
- 2 egg whites
- 2 tablespoons seedless raspberry preserves

1. Preheat the oven to 350°F and line a cupcake pan with cupcake papers.

2. To make the vanilla-raspberry cupcakes: In a mixer fitted with a paddle whip, beat the eggs and sugar in a large bowl until foamy, about 3 minutes. Add the butter and vanilla, and mix to combine. Follow with half the flour, then the milk, then the remaining flour, baking powder, and salt.

3. Pour batter into a lined cupcake pan, filling each cup slightly less than half-full. Use a spoon to make an indentation in the center of the batter, and place a heaping teaspoon of raspberry preserves in it. Cover with another tablespoon of batter, making sure not to let the jam spread out to the liner.

4. Bake for 18 to 20 minutes, until a knife inserted into the outer third of a cupcake comes out clean. Remove from the oven and allow to cool completely.

5. To make the raspberry buttercream: In a mixer fitted with a balloon whip, combine all the ingredients and beat on medium speed until totally combined, about 3 minutes.

6. Frost the cupcakes by piping the frosting through a pastry bag fitted with a decorative tip, or by spreading the frosting with a knife or spatula.

CASTIEL'S ANGEL FOOD CAKE

As we learn from characters like Metatron, Gabriel, and Michael, angels, well, they're no angels. This cake, though, is heavenly. A dozen whipped egg whites give it a light, airy body unlike any angel food cake you've ever bought from the store. Serve it with Strawberry Sauce or any kind of fresh fruit.

PREP TIME: **15 minutes**

COOK TIME: **40 minutes**

YIELD: **8 to 10 servings**

- 1 cup all-purpose flour
- 1½ cups sugar, divided
- 12 egg whites, at room temperature
- ¼ teaspoon salt
- 1½ teaspoons cream of tartar
- ½ teaspoon almond extract
- 1 teaspoon vanilla extract
- Fresh fruit, chocolate sauce, or Strawberry Sauce (page 21)

1. Preheat oven the to 350°F.

2. Combine the flour and ½ cup of the sugar in a small bowl and set aside.

3. Place the egg whites, salt, cream of tartar, and almond and vanilla extracts in the bowl of a mixer. Beat on medium with a balloon attachment until soft peaks form, then gradually add the remaining 1 cup sugar while the mixer is running, a few spoonfuls at a time, until the egg whites have become glossy white peaks, about 5 minutes. Remove from the mixer.

4. Gently fold in the flour mixture by hand with a spatula.

5. Pour the batter into an ungreased tube or Bundt pan. Bake for 35 to 40 minutes, until light golden brown.

6. Remove from the oven, invert the pan, and allow to cool for at least an hour. If the top of the cake is in danger of flattening out on the counter, place the pan on top of a long-neck bottle to hold it off the surface.

7. Run a knife around the edge of the cake once it's cool and remove from the pan. Slice and serve with fresh fruit, drizzled chocolate sauce, or Strawberry Sauce.

CROWLEY'S DEVIL'S FOOD MOUSSE

Crowley, the one-time king of hell and all-time king of the snarky nickname, refers to Sam and Dean as "Moose and Squirrel," a reference to *Rocky and Bullwinkle* and to the difference in the brothers' stature. "So, this is what you and Moose do, eh?" Crowley asks Dean. "Crisscross the country, searching for evil, order your nitrates, partake of the local attraction." He even keeps using the nicknames once he's fighting by the Winchesters' side: "Who would have thunk it, eh, Moose? You and me, same team, in the trenches. When this is over, we can get matching tattoos."

This dark chocolate mousse is a wickedly good nod to Crowley's devilish nature. The dash of almond liqueur makes it especially sinful, but feel free to change that out with orange liqueur, or raspberry, depending on your personal guilty pleasure. Serve in martini glasses for optimal indulgence.

PREP TIME: **15 minutes**
CHILL TIME: **1 hour**
YIELD: **6 to 8 servings**

- **8 ounces bittersweet chocolate**
- **4 egg whites**
- **2 tablespoons almond liqueur, divided**
- **2 tablespoons sugar**
- **2 cups heavy cream**
- **6 strawberries for garnishing**

1. Melt the chocolate over a double boiler, or in the microwave for about 90 seconds on high. Set aside.

2. Fit a mixer with a balloon whip or thin mixing blades. Put the egg whites and 1 tablespoon of almond liqueur in the bowl, and whip on high for about 3 minutes, until the egg whites are foamy. Gradually add the sugar while the mixer is running. Whip about 2 more minutes, until glossy peaks form.

3. In a large bowl, gently fold one-quarter of the egg whites into the chocolate, then fold in the rest of the egg whites. Do this carefully so that the chocolate is incorporated, but you don't lose the air from the eggs. A rubber spatula works well for this.

4. Add the cream and remaining 1 tablespoon almond liqueur to the mixing bowl, and whip on high for about 5 minutes, until stiff peaks form. Fold the whipped cream into the chocolate and egg mixture, working gently to retain as much height in the mousse as possible.

5. Spoon into individual serving dishes, cover, and refrigerate for at least 1 hour. Garnish with strawberries to serve.

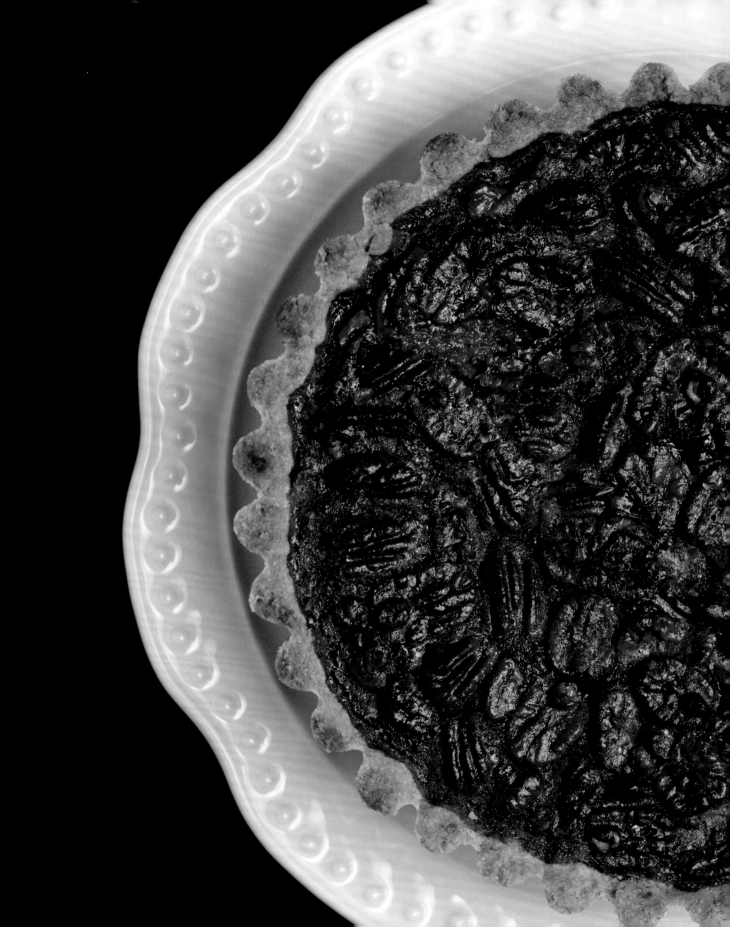

BOURBON PECAN PIE

When the Winchesters head to Carencro, Louisiana, to investigate some vampire attacks, Dean's first thought is, of course, about food. He's excited to have classic New Orleans dishes like etouffee and gumbo, but when he lands at Guidry's Cajun Café to scope out what Benny has been up to, all his cravings fly out the window in favor of pie.

"Special's pecan," Elizabeth says.

"Of course it is," Dean responds. "Let's do that."

But when she goes to get him a slice, she discovers all of the pie is gone.

"You're out of pecan," Dean says. "Story of my life."

This pie makes up for everything Dean's been missing. This recipe adds bourbon, his favorite liquor and the Southerner's unofficial drink of choice, to the classic recipe. One additional twist: a savory shortbread crust that's a perfect counterpoint to the sweet, dense filling. Keep an eye on this pie. If you're not careful, you'll run out before you know it, too.

PREP TIME:
20 minutes
COOK TIME:
40 minutes
YIELD:
8 servings

- -

SHORTBREAD CRUST
- 1 cup (2 sticks) salted butter, softened
- 2 cups all-purpose flour
- ½ cup sugar

FILLING
- 2 cups pecan halves
- 3 eggs, beaten
- 1 cup sugar
- 1 cup honey or brown rice syrup
- ¼ cup (½ stick) butter, melted
- 2 tablespoons bourbon

1. Preheat the oven to 350°F.

2. To make the shortbread crust: Mix together all the ingredients, then press into and up the sides of a 10-inch pie plate. Bake for 12 to 14 minutes, until just starting to turn golden. It won't be fully cooked. Remove from oven and allow to cool slightly.

3. Turn the oven up to 375°F.

4. Make the filling: Spread the pecans on the bottom of the pie crust. Mix together the remaining ingredients and pour over the pecans. Bake about 40 minutes, until just set in the middle. Remove from the oven and let cool completely.

SWEET CHERRY PIE

"Cherry Pie," the hair metal classic by Warrant, is the soundtrack to Dean's dreams—literally. He once has a dream where two women, one dressed as an angel and one dressed as a demon, give him a private dance to the song. "Tastes so good make a grown man cry," the song goes. "Sweet cherry pie."

This pie might not bring you to tears, but it will definitely gather everyone around the table. Fresh cherries are even better than frozen in this recipe, but if they're out of season, you'll have a hard time finding them. You can also use tart cherries and add ¼ cup more sugar. Serve with whipped cream and a healthy dose of '80s rock.

PREP TIME:
15 minutes

COOK TIME:
60 minutes

YIELD:
8 servings

- **2 prepared pie crusts**
- **5 cups frozen pitted sweet cherries, thawed and drained**
- **½ cup plus 2 tablespoons sugar**
- **½ cup flour**
- **¼ cup cornstarch**
- **Juice of ½ lemon**
- **1 teaspoon vanilla extract**
- **1 teaspoon almond extract**
- **1 egg, beaten**
- **1 tablespoon milk**

1. Preheat the oven to 350°F.

2. Lay one of the pie crusts in a 9-inch pie pan, making sure the dough lays flat to the bottom and sides.

3. In a large bowl, combine the cherries, ½ cup of the sugar, flour, cornstarch, lemon juice, and vanilla and almond extracts. Mix well. Pour the fruit into the crust in the pan. Lay the other pie crust on top, firmly crimping the edges together with your fingers or a fork. Cut vents in the top of the dough, in a decorative shape if you like.

4. Combine the egg and milk in a small bowl. Brush the top crust with the mixture, then sprinkle with the remaining 2 tablespoons sugar.

5. Bake for 20 minutes at 350°F, then raise the temperature to 400°F and bake for another 30 to 35 minutes, until the crust is golden brown. Remove from the oven and allow the pie to cool for at least 2 hours before serving to let the filling set.

COCONUT CREAM PIE

When Sam and Dean are on the case in Prosperity, Indiana, they're trying to stop a vengeful witch who's hexing the town. Dean's alone in the motel room, about to dig into a giant cream pie straight from the tin, when Sam walks in. "Dude, pie!" Dean says, before Sam drops a giant bag of chicken feet on the table. "It's like the town ran out of luck," Sam reports one resident as saying. Dean ran out of luck, too: The power outages and burst pipes meant the chicken feet they needed were rancid, so he lost his appetite, even for pie.

This Southern Coconut Cream Pie is so sweet and delicious that you're going to want to eat it right from the pan, too. Both the coconut custard and whipped cream topping get a little kick from coconut rum, but if you'd rather leave the booze out, just substitute coconut extract.

PREP TIME:
25 minutes

COOK TIME:
60 minutes

YIELD:
**8 servings
(or 1 Dean
Winchester)**

. . . .

CUSTARD PIE

- **One 8-inch prepared graham cracker crust**
- **1 cup plus 3 tablespoons shredded coconut**
- **½ cup granulated sugar**
- **¼ cup cornstarch**
- **2 cups milk**
- **4 egg yolks**
- **2 tablespoons butter**
- **1 tablespoon coconut rum or 1 teaspoon coconut extract**

WHIPPED CREAM TOPPING

- **2 cups heavy cream**
- **1 tablespoon coconut rum or 1 teaspoon coconut extract**
- **¼ cup confectioners' sugar**
- **1 teaspoon powdered gelatin**

1. Preheat the oven to 375°F.

2. To make the custard pie: Bake the pie crust for 5 minutes, or according to package directions, until golden brown. Set aside to cool.

3. Spread 3 tablespoons of the shredded coconut on a baking sheet, and toast in the oven until golden brown, about 8 minutes. Set aside to cool.

4. Combine the granulated sugar and cornstarch in a medium saucepan over medium heat. Whisk in the milk and egg yolks, and cook, stirring constantly, until the custard thickens. This takes about 5 minutes, but will thicken in an instant, so make sure to keep a close eye on the pan. Remove from the heat, stir in the butter, rum or coconut extract, and the remaining 1 cup shredded coconut, then cover and chill for 30 minutes.

5. Transfer the custard to the pie crust, cover, and refrigerate at least 30 minutes (longer is better) until the pie is set.

6. Prepare the whipped cream topping: Place the cream and rum or coconut extract in the bowl of a mixer fitted with a balloon whip. Combine the confectioners' sugar and gelatin in a measuring cup. (The gelatin will help the whipped cream stay whipped longer. If you're serving the pie immediately, you can omit it.) Beat the cream on medium-high, gradually adding the sugar mixture, until stiff peaks form.

7. Spread the whipped cream over the custard, and top with the toasted coconut. Serve on plates or eat it right from the pan—no judgment here.

BLUEBERRY PIE

"I will pick us up some grub, and unlike you Sam, I will not forget the pie," Charlie once says. Even when the pie isn't cursed or made by zombies, something happens—usually Sam—that keeps Dean away from his pie. "Look at these chemicals!" Sam once says.

"Do you even read the label?"

"No, I read pie," Dean responds. "The rest is just blah, blah, blah."

There are exceptions, though, like one meal he and Sam share with Mary Winchester when she comes back from the dead. "Do you still like pie?" she asks Dean. He can barely answer, "I mean, uh . . ." before he dives into the blueberry pie she brought for him.

When this pie is ready to eat, you're probably going to do the same thing. The bright zing of lemon really complements the fresh fruit. (If you're using frozen, make sure to thaw and drain the berries well.) The two hours of waiting between this pie coming out of the oven and when it's ready to serve will be the hardest you'll ever spend. But if you can make it to the other side, your reward is this amazing dessert.

PREP TIME:
10 minutes
CHILL TIME:
45 minutes
YIELD:
8 servings

- **2 prepared pie crusts**
- **4 cups blueberries**
- **¾ cup sugar**
- **2 tablespoons all-purpose flour**
- **2 tablespoons cornstarch**
- **Juice of ½ lemon**
- **Pinch of salt**
- **1 egg, beaten**
- **1 tablespoon milk**

1. Preheat the oven to 375°F.

2. Lay one of the pie crusts in the pie pan, making sure the dough lays flat to the bottom and sides.

3. In a large bowl, combine the blueberries, sugar, flour, cornstarch, lemon juice, and salt. Mix well. Pour the fruit into the crust in the pan.

4. Lay the other pie crust flat on a floured surface. Using a knife or pizza cutter, cut the dough into ¾-inch strips. Lay them over the top of the fruit in a crisscross pattern.

5. Combine the egg and milk in a small bowl. Brush the top crust with the mixture, and bake until the fruit is bubbling and the crust is golden brown, 40 to 45 minutes.

6. Remove from the oven and allow to cool for at least 2 hours before cutting to allow the filling to set.

PUDDING!

At first, Dean thinks Sam's idea of getting themselves admitted to a mental hospital in "Sam, Interrupted" to help fellow hunter Martin is a crazy idea. "All right Nurse Ratched," he says to the nurse giving his entrance exam, "I've seen *Cuckoo's Nest*, so don't try any of your soul-crushing authoritarian crap on me." But in no time, he's acting the part. When a staff member catches the brothers investigating a body in the morgue, Dean stages a distraction, dropping his pants and yelling, "Pudding!"

This from-scratch butterscotch pudding comes together in minutes and tastes incredible. Just make sure to stir continuously while it's cooking: The pudding will cook for a long time and then hit its thickening point in just a second, and needs to be removed from the heat immediately when it does.

PREP TIME:
15 minutes

CHILL TIME:
1 hour

YIELD:
6 servings

• •

- **3 cups whole milk**
- **4 egg yolks**
- **1 teaspoon vanilla extract**
- **1 cup loosely packed dark brown sugar**
- **¼ cup cornstarch**
- **½ teaspoon salt**
- **¼ cup (½ stick) butter**

1. In a small bowl, whisk together the milk, egg yolks, and vanilla.

2. In a medium saucepan over medium heat, combine the brown sugar, cornstarch, and salt. Whisk in the wet ingredients, and bring to a boil, stirring constantly.

3. Just as the pudding starts to boil, it should quickly thicken. As soon as it does, remove the pan from the heat and whisk in the butter.

4. Pour into individual serving bowls, cover, and refrigerate until set, at least an hour.

CHAPTER 7

DRINKS

. . . .

For the Winchesters, alcohol serves a lot of different purposes. It's a way to loosen lips during investigations, and for Dean, a way to meet the ladies. It's also a coping mechanism to deal with all their losses, battles, and brushes with mortality. These cocktails aren't meant to be downed to drown your sorrows after a bad day fighting monsters. They're easy-to-make, easy-to-savor libations that add a touch of *spirit* to a celebration.

JACK'S BREAKFAST CEREAL MILKSHAKE

Jack—a Nephilim, the son of Lucifer and a human—didn't exactly have a normal childhood. His mother died when he was born, and he went from infant to young adult in the blink of an eye. Though he's learning to navigate the world as a grown-up (and a force of good), Jack still has a few kid-like behaviors: namely, his love of sugary breakfast cereal. When Castiel catches Jack eating cereal in the middle of the night, Jack says, "Don't tell Sam." "It's the middle of the night," Cas says. "I couldn't wait until morning," Jack responds. "Sam says this stuff will rot your teeth, but I like it." This milkshake has the best of both worlds—childlike nostalgia from cereal, and an adult kick from spirits. Enjoy it for dessert or for breakfast. No judgment here.

PREP TIME:
5 minutes
YIELD:
1 serving

- **2 cups vanilla ice cream**
- **½ cup milk**
- **½ cup sweet breakfast cereal, plus more for garnishing**
- **2 ounces vanilla vodka (optional)**
- **Whipped cream for topping**

1. Combine the ice cream, milk, cereal, and vodka, if using, in a blender and blend until smooth.

2. Pour into a tall glass, top with whipped cream, and garnish with more cereal.

GARY'S BANANA DAIQUIRI

When Sam sidles up to the bar at the beginning of "Swap Meat," it's clear that something is amiss.

"Evening, barkeep," he says. **"I would like to purchase an alcohol, please."**

"What can I get you?" the bartender asks.

"Well, I'm 26, as you can see from my license," Sam replies.

"Uh huh," the bartender says, unimpressed. **"What can I get you?"**

"A banana daiquiri, my good man."

It turns out the thing that's wrong with Sam is that he isn't actually Sam: He's Gary, a nerdy teenager who cast a body-swapping spell. The banana daiquiri he drinks, though, is totally real and totally refreshing, especially by a pool on a hot day. Feel free to add or subtract fruit—like more pineapple and less coconut—to suit your taste.

PREP TIME:
5 minutes
YIELD:
1 serving

. . . .

- 1 small banana
- 2 tablespoons cream of coconut
- 2 tablespoons pineapple juice
- Juice of ½ lime
- 2 ounces light rum

1. In a blender, combine all the ingredients, and fill halfway with ice.

2. Blend until smooth.

ROWENA'S POTION

Rowena isn't just the most powerful witch in the world—she's also the best dressed. This potion might not have any magical powers, but it *does* pack quite a punch. A riff on a New York sour that uses Scotch to honor Rowena's heritage, this drink has a float of red wine that swirls through the rest of the glass, making for an entrancing show. Actually, maybe it does have a magical power after all: It will make you come back for more time and time again.

PREP TIME:
5 minutes
YIELD:
1 serving

GINGER SIMPLE SYRUP

- 1 cup water
- 1 tablespoon finely chopped fresh ginger
- 1 cup sugar

COCKTAIL

- 2 ounces blended Scotch
- 1 ounce fresh lemon juice
- 1 ounce ginger simple syrup
- 1 ounce Cabernet Sauvignon or other red wine

1. To make the simple syrup: Boil the water in a small saucepan, then add the ginger and sugar. Boil for 5 minutes, then remove from the heat and cover. Allow to steep for 1 hour (longer will result in a stronger ginger flavor). Strain.

2. To make the cocktail: Combine the Scotch, lemon juice, and ginger simple syrup in a shaker with ice. Shake until chilled.

3. Pour into a rocks glass over ice.

4. Gently pour the red wine into the glass so the wine stays at the top.

MEN OF LETTERS OLD-FASHIONED

An ancient secret organization, the Men of Letters are "preceptors, observers, beholders, chroniclers" of unexplainable mysteries and supernatural phenomena.

Generations of Winchesters were Men of Letters, including Sam and Dean's grandfather Henry Winchester, who, in 1958, was forced to give up his family while battling a formidable demon.

Just like the Men of Letters, the old-fashioned is a classic institution. This variation on the cocktail includes a little bit of a modern twist, with the addition of an amaro (try Montenegro) and some gourmet bitters, but is still made in the classic, old-fashioned way.

PREP TIME:
5 minutes
YIELD:
1 serving

- 1½ ounces rye whiskey
- ¼ ounce amaro
- 2 dashes orange bitters
- 1 dash walnut bitters
- Orange peel, 2 for garnishing

1. In a rocks glass, combine all the ingredients except the orange peel.

2. Stir gently with a cocktail spoon. Add a large ice cube or ice sphere.

3. Garnish with orange peel.

HUNTER'S EGGNOG

Hunters also need to stop and celebrate every now and then, even if they're doing it while investigating family members being pulled up the chimney by a mysterious "evil Santa," as Sam theorizes, and get captured by a pair of pagan gods who attempt to eat them. In "A Very Supernatural Christmas," the brothers manage to escape, of course, and go back to their hotel room to drink eggnog and exchange gifts they bought at the gas mart down the street.

This creamy, Christmas-y treat is much better than what you can get at the gas station (or the grocery store) and is surprisingly easy to make.

PREP TIME:
20 minutes

COOK TIME:
2 hours or overnight

YIELD:
8 servings

- **4 cups milk**
- **2 teaspoons ground cinnamon, divided**
- **1 teaspoon ground nutmeg**
- **½ teaspoon ground ginger**
- **12 egg yolks**
- **1 cup sugar**
- **2 cups heavy cream**
- **¾ cup bourbon**

1. In a large saucepan over medium heat, combine the milk, 1 teaspoon of the cinnamon, and the nutmeg and ginger. Slowly bring to a gentle boil. Remove from the heat.

2. In a medium bowl, whisk the egg yolks and sugar together. Slowly whisk in the hot mixture, a little at a time, to temper the eggs so they don't cook.

3. Return the mixture to the pan and cook over medium heat until the mixture thickens but doesn't boil, about 8 minutes.

4. Remove from the heat and stir in the heavy cream and bourbon.

5. Refrigerate until completely cool. This drink improves if you let it sit overnight and will keep for a few days, so the longer you let it set, the better.

ROCKY'S BAR MARGARITA

In "Nihilism," Michael has Dean trapped inside Rocky's Bar, a place in his own mind where Dean will stay happy and quiet while the archangel carries out his evil plan. Inside the bar, Dean plays the same loop over and over: cutting limes to make the house special—tequila shots. "We're not making the house special without limes," he says.

"What are we, savages?"

While it isn't a tequila shot, this cocktail is so simple and easy that it practically takes the same amount of preparation. This margarita uses fresh lime juice, tequila, a little bit of orange liqueur and salt, and it's so good that you might never need to buy another bottle of margarita mix again. For an interesting twist, swap the tequila with smoky mezcal and add a squeeze of fresh orange juice.

PREP TIME:
5 minutes
YIELD:
1 serving

- **2 ounces tequila or mezcal**
- **Juice of 1 lime**
- **Squeeze of orange juice (optional)**
- **½ ounce orange liqueur**
- **Salt for the rim**

1. Combine the tequila or mezcal, lime juice, orange juice, and orange liqueur in a shaker with ice. Shake to chill.

2. Run a cut lime around the edge of a margarita glass and dip the rim in salt to coat.

3. Pour the liquid into the glass over ice.

CARRY ON, WAYWARD SONS

After 15 seasons, Sam and Dean are hanging up their fake government IDs to head to greener, less supernatural pastures. Why not celebrate their farewell with a Winchester feast? Start with an appetizer spread that would put craft services to shame—put out several options, and definitely don't skip the pretzels with beer cheese. Then serve the legendary Winchester Surprise. For dessert, go all pie, especially Dean's favorites, cherry and blueberry. Raise a toast with any of the cocktails in this book or just with a Winchester-approved beer or two.

ABOUT THE AUTHOR

Julie Tremaine is a food and travel writer whose work has appeared in outlets such as Forbes.com, Bloomberg Next, SyFy Wire, *Yankee*, and *Providence Monthly*, where she was executive editor and creative director. Julie doesn't like to take sides in the Team Sam or Team Dean debate . . . because she's Team Castiel. Read more of her writing at Travel-Sip-Repeat.com

ABOUT THE PHOTOGRAPHER

Jessica Torres is a freelance photographer based in her hometown of Los Angeles, California. Jessica fell in love with photography at a young age, getting her hands on any available camera. Her time working in the hospitality industry led her down her path in food and beverage photography. She enjoys exploring new flavors and capturing them visually to share with others.

AUTHOR ACKNOWLEDGMENTS

One day, on a flight from the East Coast to the West, I sent an email to an editor, literally on a wing and a prayer, and this book is what happened. Thank you to Kelly Reed at Insight Editions for entrusting me with this project. It was an honor and a privilege to create a real-life version of the Winchester diet. I couldn't have done it without photographer Jessica Torres, who, from a lucky meeting at a bar in downtown Los Angeles, made these ideas a reality. Thanks to everyone who lovingly (and bravely) ate early versions while I cooked this book into existence, and to the best lady friends for bringing wine to my dinner parties and being my first and most supportive tasters. Thank you, especially, to Beth-Anne, Lexie and Sergei, and Gabriel, for all the other dreams you've helped make come true.

INSIGHT EDITIONS

PO Box 3088
San Rafael, CA 94912
www.insighteditions.com

f Find us on Facebook: www.facebook.com/InsightEditions
🐦 Follow us on Twitter: @insighteditions

Publisher: Raoul Goff
President: Kate Jerome
Associate Publisher: Vanessa Lopez
Creative Director: Chrissy Kwasnik
Designer: Evelyn Furuta
Senior Editor: Kelly Reed
Editorial Assistant: Gabriela Vanacore
Managing Editor: Lauren LePera
Production Editor: Jennifer Bentham
Production Director/Subsidiary Rights: Lina s Palma
Senior Production Manager: Greg Steffen
Production Coordinator: Eden Orlesky
Front Cover Photography: Ted Thomas
Front Cover Food and Prop Styling: Elena P Craig

ROOTS of PEACE   🌱 REPLANTED PAPER

Insight Editions, in association with Roots of Peace, will plant two trees for each tree used in
the manufacturing of this book. Roots of Peace is an internationally renowned humanitarian
organization dedicated to eradicating land mines worldwide and converting war-torn lands
into productive farms and wildlife habitats. Roots of Peace will plant two million fruit and nut
trees in Afghanistan and provide farmers there with the skills and support necessary for
sustainable land use.

Manufactured in China by Insight Editions

10 9 8 7 6